HOW TO RIDE THE
SUBWAY

Getting Around on
Wall Street and in Life

JIMMY LEBENTHAL

A REGALO PRESS BOOK
ISBN: 979-8-89565-198-8
ISBN (eBook): 979-8-89565-199-5

How to Ride the Subway:
Getting Around on Wall Street and in Life
© 2026 by Jimmy Lebenthal
All Rights Reserved

Cover Design by Conroy Accord
Cover Photo by Markus Pizzini

Publishing Team:
Founder and Publisher – Gretchen Young
Managing Editor – Caitlin Burdette
Production Manager – Brynlee Wolfe
Production Editor – Rachel Paul

Regalo Press
New York • Nashville
regalopress.com

Published in the United States of America
1 2 3 4 5 6 7 8 9 10

Table of Contents

Introduction

The Coldest Eyeball in New York City

THAT'S WHAT RELATIVES WHO knew me as a young boy called me. Was I a late-twentieth-century urban reincarnation of Billy the Kid? Or a precocious arctic explorer? No, its origin traces back to when I was six years old, and my father took me down to visit his office in the Financial District of Lower Manhattan. While I had been to his office before, these had always been weekend visits and we would drive down the West Side Highway—the old, decrepit elevated West Side Highway that literally collapsed one day in 1973 under the weight of a truck. At the time of our drives to work, the elevated highway provided a prominent view of a still-working New York City waterfront. Cruise ships, cargo ships, and occasional warships lined the plentiful wharfs along 12th Avenue. But then one weekday we went by subway—the New

York City Metropolitan Transportation Authority's (MTA's) 7th Avenue IRT line—and so began a lifelong fascination.

Now, I realize that many of you are probably rolling your eyes, thinking, "The New York City Subway?" That smelly, noisy, dangerous hole in the ground? Surely, you jest! And even more to the point, surely a man of your stature and accomplishments would aspire to greater sources of travel inspiration. Perhaps a limo? A Maybach? A helicopter or private jet? No, none of those could ever hold sway over my imagination the way the NYC Subway did and still does.

The excitement for me started as soon as we reached the platform. Looking down the long tunnel leading north from the 96th Street Station, I saw the distant eyes of some unknown beast turn the corner half a mile down the dark tube. The lights of the approaching subway were still dim but I could tell they were rushing towards us. What would they bring? It felt like a mythical beast was hurtling at me. Would it be danger—should I run back up the stairs? Or would it be opportunity, adventure, excitement? The great din and rush of air when it entered the station was only the start of the adventure.

We boarded the first car of the Express. Back in those days, the train operator sat in a small enclosed booth to the side at the front of the car and there was a window in the middle of the front door through which an excited boy could watch the journey unfold. And what a journey it was! It was all so new to me. Rolling along the tracks, the steel supports blurred in my vision, passing the Local stations, twisting and turning through the tunnels. After that trip, I looked for every opportunity I could to take the subway. I would drag whoever was with me to the front end of the station and eagerly await the coming voyage that loomed like a rocket trip through the solar system.

The only issue was that I was not very tall. I could see all this through the lower edge of the front window if I stood on my tippy toes, but that got tiresome after a while. The solution quickly revealed itself. Below the window was a keyhole at a convenient height for me. I could look with one eye through that lens and see all. The air would rush right onto my eye as the train progressed, which led my father and other family members to proclaim that I must have "the coldest eyeball in New York City."

Photo Credits: Adam E. Moreira, R38R40, Erik Calonius

Fascination with the subways blossomed in many ways. I learned which stations had switchboards visible from the platform, from which you could track the trains as a bystander. Abandoned stations enthralled me. Why had a 91st Street Station ever existed on the 7th Avenue IRT, when there was a 96th Street Station and an 86th Street Station? On Broadway's sidewalks above could I see the outline of where the entrance had been? The bridge to Track 4 of the Times Square Shuttle was actually in the tunnel that the Local train rumbled on. You could reach out and almost touch it as it went past. All the while, every train I took, I made sure to get in the front car. I imagine mine was the same thrill as that of a cave explorer: Every curve taken in the tunnel, every dip or rise in the tracks carried anticipation of a fascinating new subterranean landscape on its other side.

Friends of mine growing up knew this strange affinity I had for the subterranean lair. I had piles of old subway maps that I would pore over and memorize. Even today, and with the miracle that is the internet, I sometimes scour online maps of the subway system, now much more intricate, with detailed track configurations and station layouts.

In the roughly fifty years since the day of that first fateful ride, the subway has factored into my life in many ways. To start with, my father was a prominent underwriter, salesman, and promoter of municipal bonds, which were used to build and maintain the NYC Subway system. Many of his commercials featured the subways for the amazing efficiency and low cost by which they enabled workers to get to and from their jobs. The efficiency and productivity enhancements of subways were often a dinner conversation topic. Then there were the various friendships that depended on subways in one way or another: to get to sporting events, extracurricular activities, and so on. And dear family members—none more so than my beloved cousin Annie—with whom I would take the subway to myriad New York City institutions, such as Coney Island's amusement park, the Ringling Bros. and Barnum & Bailey Circus at Madison Square Garden, and the Bronx Zoo.

In my adult life, I have had plenty of subway experiences outside of New York, and I will share these experiences with you in the pages that follow. But why should you bother to indulge my idiosyncratic childhood memories by reading this book? Well, the subway is analogous to other important aspects of my life. Many people know me as a businessman and investor through my regular CNBC appearances. With this book, I hope to give deeper insight into how I became who I am. I hope to use my stories from the subway as metaphors and lessons for becoming successful at investing and forming positive habits in the workplace. With each chapter, I share a story from the subway and use it to illustrate what I've learned that has gotten me through life in the markets and in corporate life.

My infatuation with subways coincided with another childhood passion: investing in stocks. It was not only my father who worked in finance. My grandparents started the family municipal bond firm in 1926. Through the '70s, '80s, and '90s, my father was its chief executive officer, and my grandmother was its chairman. My Aunt Ellie and Uncle

Gerry both worked there. My siblings and I, as well as our cousins, spent summers interning there. The family business and municipal finance were in our DNA. For me, though, the allure of investing in stocks grabbed hold early. It may have been the stock tables that drew me in. Those dozen or so tiny-font pages in the back of the newspaper—print, mind you, this was well before the internet—with the hieroglyphics of the previous day's trading. Hi-lo-close, New York Stock Exchange, American Stock Exchange, over-the-counter, highest volume, up a quarter, down three-eighths—it was all a puzzle that I knew I wanted to work out. I recognized that I could put my brain power to work and make money. But how?

At the age of twelve, I asked my dad for ten shares of Texaco, Inc. and ten shares of United States Shoe Corporation for Christmas. I didn't know what I was doing, and I cannot remember how I landed on those two names. But the hook was set. Every morning I would retrieve the newspaper before anyone else woke up to check where my two stocks had closed the day before. Again, this was well before the internet; if you wanted an intraday quote, you had to call a broker to get it. My early attempts at doing that were soon met with a response of "Hey, kid, are you gonna trade or what?" So, I would find out the next day. But this was only the start. I had to find out what was making these stock prices move. The two names had different runs. Texaco, the oil company, was locked in a legal dispute with Getty Oil that held the share price back. It wasn't much fun to track the ups and downs of a court case instead of how the business of exploring for, producing, and marketing energy was going. US Shoe was a different story.

US Shoe made shoe-manufacturing equipment. In the early 1980s it started to gain more and more market share. Its shares rose, management split the shares, and then split the shares again and again and again. My ten shares rapidly became a much larger number. The share price rose, dividends went up, and I relished getting any mail from the company, most of which was dividend checks and certificates for more shares.

In my current stage of life, I sometimes look back at the principles that got me where I am today. The parallels between the lessons of how to ride the subway and how to invest are many. And they are not the only parallels. To succeed in business requires interpersonal skills. So does safely and efficiently using the subway.

Preteen and teenage years in 1980s New York were a phenomenon unto itself. Picture a Norman Rockwell painting, and then picture its exact opposite. Students from Manhattan's prep-school culture at the time know of what I write. That life molded me into the man I am. I didn't understand the lessons I was learning at the time. There is a lot to be said for the unique—some might say dorky—literary technique of using the subway as metaphor for investing and for getting along with people. It is all mine, though, and it reflects the way that I have sought to forge bonds in the workplace, be it in the Navy, the financial industry, or the media.

Morality is not a part of the equation in this book. While I happen to believe that when entering a subway car one should "step aside and let the passengers off the train first," as the announcement goes, I am aware that there are on occasion legitimate reasons why someone might rush to board. I am not writing this to pronounce judgments. In investing, there are ways to transact that are not my cup of tea but which serve a purpose. Short-selling stocks and the price discovery it entails come to mind. And in business, while I have learned that an informed opinion, gently delivered, is my preferred way to act, there are others for whom bombast does the trick. Yes, I will tell you how I endeavor to act and how the subway has helped to teach me. But by no means I am wrapping myself in a cloak of righteousness. With these anecdotes I intend to show how I have been successful as an investor, businessman, and New York City commuter. And, more than just successful: how I've learned to enjoy each of those spheres in my life.

A helpful way to think about this book is to watch the courtroom scene from the classic military justice movie *A Few Good Men*. If you haven't seen it, I humbly offer the opinion that it is a must-see for the acting and script. At one point, the lance corporal on trial is asked by the prosecutor to find the definition of "code red" in the *Marine Outline for Recruit Training*. Code red is the term for the extrajudicial punishment that the corporal and his squad mate meted out on an underperforming platoon mate. Being an informal term, the defendant confesses that it is not in the manual or any other official document, implying the action was unsanctioned. Seeming to have made his point, the smirking prosecutor rests and allows counsel for the defense to counter. The defense attorney grabs the manual from the prosecutor and approaches the witness box. Here is their dialogue.

> Defense Attorney, Lieutenant Junior Grade (LTJG) Kaffee: Corporal, would you turn to the page in this book that says where the mess hall is, please?
>
> Defendant Corporal (Cpl.) Barnes: Well, Lt. Kaffee, that's not in the book, sir.
>
> LTJG Kaffee: You mean to say in all your time at Gitmo, you've never had a meal?
>
> Cpl. Barnes: No, sir. Three squares a day, sir.
>
> LTJG Kaffee: I don't understand. How did you know where the mess hall was if it's not in this book?
>
> Cpl. Barnes: Well, I guess I just followed the crowd at chow time, sir.
>
> LTJG Kaffee: No more questions.

Much like the young hayseed of a corporal, the average rider of the New York City Subway system knows that to use the underground railway requires far more intuition than the instructions listed on the MetroCard machine.

Photo Credits: Jim Lebenthal

There are unwritten rules and ways to ride the subway efficiently. Not only that, these rules are metaphors for being successful in investments and business. Plenty of ink has been spilled on these topics. Some of what I write may seem intuitively obvious. My hope is that through the prism of a subway ride, they may take on more meaning and importance for the reader. Further, I hope you will enjoy getting to know me a bit better.

I ride the subway many times a week. It is the fastest way for me to get from my Midtown office to the CNBC set at the New York Stock Exchange. An hour-long car ride is reduced to twenty-five minutes door to door. Each and every time I enter a subway station, I feel the same excitement I felt on my first ride at age six. Many people ride the subway every day. I hope that in the same quotidian way that the subway serves our commuting needs, these stories will provide a basis for day-to-day life as an investor, a business person, and a decent human being in the world.

As I write, the New York City Subway is engulfed in controversy. An ugly wave of crime is gripping the system, making life increasingly dangerous for its riders. Unlike in the 1970s and 1980s in which I grew up, this is not economic crime, that of the underprivileged seeking wealthy targets to rob. It is a more sinister streak of violence, fueled by mental illness and social disorder. It is typified by horrifying acts of violence. Also echoing the late twentieth century, the subway system is chronically underfunded, leading to decaying infrastructure and rider delays. Its reputation is on a slide. I am happy to write this book, in part as a paean to the subway that I truly love and in which I find perpetual amazement.

Let me also share an important concept. Much of life is learning by doing. I enjoy sharing with you the lessons I've learned, but believe me, I've learned them the hard way. I've been mugged in the subway, I've made a few horrible investment choices in my career, and, unfortunately, I have some vignettes from my work life that I cringe to think about. The old saying—good judgment comes from experience; experience comes from bad judgment—is writ large in my case. That's not a bug in the program of life. It is a feature. Despite difficult moments along the way, I live every day excited, energized, and inspired by every investment decision, business move, and subway ride.

With that, I hear the clickety-clack and screech of metal wheels on steel rails. Let's begin our journey!

Chapter 1

Know Where You Are Going

THE SUBWAY IS A conveyance, a means to efficiently get from point A to point B. As such, it is one of many forms of transportation. In deciding to take the subway instead of, say, a bus or a car, it is vital to know where you are going. If you're going from the West Side to the East Side in Manhattan, a subway is likely not your best bet. It will entail at least two different subway lines and the 42nd Street Shuttle, or perhaps a third line to complete the journey. A trip to an airport can be done by subway, although New York City's subway system is depressingly inefficient for this, requiring a bus transfer to get to LaGuardia and a separate, additional trip on the AirTrain to reach JFK. Newark Airport is completely out, as far as getting there by subway is concerned, since the Metropolitan Transportation Authority (MTA) has not crossed the mile-wide Hudson River.

If, however, you want to get from your Upper Manhattan home to your Midtown or Financial District office, the subway is marvelous. Stations are generally spaced a short, convenient distance from each other, making the journey's start easy. The trains come often and continuously. You don't need to consult a timetable or wonder if the subway has closed for the night. And as the subway cars travel underground, they avoid the legendary traffic that often congests Manhattan, as any cab rider can confirm. That traffic will only grow over time, with the ever-increasing number of NYC streets being rebranded as pedestrian plazas.

Similarly, for many major sporting events in New York City, the subway is fabulously more convenient, and a hell of a lot cheaper, than driving or taking a cab. Yankee Stadium, Citi Field, Madison Square Garden, and the National Tennis Center are examples. And many cultural and recreational spots are best reached by subway. The Bronx Zoo, the Botanical Garden, and Coney Island come to mind. You don't have to worry about whether you will find a parking lot or how expensive one might be. Tolls, gas, and wear and tear on your car all fall by the wayside. And while some may find subway crowds off-putting, to me they pale in comparison to the combat-level experience that is driving a car in New York City. Plus, the camaraderie of fans on a subway can be a heck of a good time!

In short, the subway can be incredible useful, but only if you know where you're going. The same is true in investing and in business.

There are many, many different types of investment philosophies. Embracing one of these philosophies is akin to knowing where you are going. Fundamental investing, technical analysis, momentum trading, and risk arbitrage are just some of a very long list. It is vital—vital!—that an investor identify his methodology ahead of time. Just as the subway can be a terrible means to visit the Metropolitan Museum of Art from the Upper West Side, so too can fundamental analysis be the wrong path if you don't intend to read annual reports, study financial statements, interview company managements, and so on. I use that example because probably the biggest mistake that I see people make in investing is thinking they are capable of evaluating the long-term prospects for a business or industry without doing the time-consuming intellectual work to prove it. If unwilling or unable to do that work, an investor has many other investment styles from which to choose. Just as the M96, M86, and M79 buses are fabulous ways to travel crosstown in Manhattan, much easier than taking a subway, so too passive exchange-traded funds (ETF) investing may be better suited for where some investors want to go. The major investment philosophies need not compete with one another, just like different transportation modes don't need to. But knowing where you are going as an investor is as vital as knowing where you are going as a subway or bus rider.

So, start by defining what your destination is. Are you looking for long-term results that take advantage of the tax-deferred nature of gains that comes from selling only after long holding periods? If so, a more fundamental analytical approach, one that tries to determine the intrinsic value of a company in relation to its current share price, may be your preferred path. As anyone who has spoken to me about investments knows, this is my passion in the stock market. Intrinsic value means what a company might be worth if it were purchased entirely by a third party in a take-private transaction. If you feel confident in your calculations, and you see that the company is trading at 70 percent, 60 percent, or 50 percent of that value in the public markets, well, there is your opportunity. The payoffs to such investing can be large. The primary risk is, of course, that your analysis can be off. You may misestimate the competitive landscape, or the industry may be undergoing a sea change, both of which may seismically alter the intrinsic value. But the most pernicious risk can be that you sometimes must wait a long time in a fundamental investment. This risk is result of the fact that your purchase of a company's shares does nothing in and of itself to unlock that intrinsic value. The racehorses are not released from the gate at the sound of your purchase. The act of waiting can be hard, especially when other stocks can be on moonshots and you feel like you are missing out. I write in Chapter 3 about patience and in Chapter 7 about the dangers of overtrading. Suffice it for now to say that these risks are best managed by knowing where you are going—what type of investor you are—before you start your journey. That way, you don't stray from the course.

In the past ten years, my style of investing has not been the favorite. Price sensitivity, business analysis, and management competence should always be important stock-picking criteria. But for most of the post–financial crisis era, growth-at-any-cost investing has been preferred. Fundamental analysis can eventually lead to these sorts of investments. I was a latecomer to AI-semiconductor manufacturer Nvidia, for instance, buying it in 2023 after it had already had a marvelous run. Until that point, it had seemed wildly overpriced to many. But my purchase tripled in one year because, even though I waited until its valuation justified its business merits, the combination of both left plenty of gains ahead. Still, for most of the investments I've made in the past decade, I've had to wait longer than expected to reach the destination of a great return. Sometimes that wait has been hard, especially in the fiery heat of the public cauldron that is CNBC, where the merits—and demerits—of my willingness to wait often are debated by my peers.

In another example, I waited a long time before making my first purchase of Amazon in 2024. The awe-inspiring merits of the company had been unquestionable for years. The stock price valuation, however, left much to be desired in my opinion, especially after the COVID-19-era runup when everyone sat home and ordered from Amazon, giving the shares a boost. When I first purchased AMZN shares, it was at the same price they traded in the spring of 2020, almost four years earlier. Sticking to my discipline—knowing who I am and where I am going as an investor—meant paying attention to the intrinsic value of the company and how that related to the current trading price. In 2020 it simply didn't have a discount to its intrinsic value. In 2024, however, after a three-year period in which it grew sales and net income by more than 50 percent, and trading at the same share price as four years earlier, the timing of that purchase was excellent. In the following six months, the stock returned 20 percent and I think it has more gains ahead.

As you are reading, you may be thinking, "Gee, Jimmy, that's nice that you've had those investing experiences, but how can I look for the same opportunities?" I'm glad you asked. While other investment styles may look for strong momentum or breakneck revenue growth, fundamental analysis tries to determine what the basic earnings power of a company is. It then derives how much of those earnings need to be plowed back into the business to keep it running (buying new airplanes if you're an airline, for example, or maintaining factories if you're a manufacturer) and thus, how much of those earnings are left over for you, as the shareholder, to enjoy. The latter is an approximate description of free cash flow (FCF). FCF can benefit shareholders in many ways. It can be used to buy back shares, pay dividends, reinvest in expanding the business, pay down debt, or make strategic acquisitions, all of which are activities with the potential to boost share prices.

Identifying the level of current and future earnings is half the battle.

Once you've done so, you have to decide how much you are willing to pay for those cash flows. Often, I speak on air and to clients about the "PEG" ratio (price/earnings-to-growth ratio). No pricing methodology is foolproof, but using the PEG ratio consistently keeps me from overpaying for cash flows. The PEG ratio is simply the current price-to-earnings ratio of a stock (its current share price divided by its earning per share) divided by the future annual growth rate of those earnings per share. The numerator is objective, a pure measurement. The denominator is where discretion comes in. And not just any discretion: This is where the art of valuing businesses becomes the science. The growth rate that you project for earnings plays a huge role in determining their worth. Is thirty-five times forward earnings too expensive? Maybe not for Nvidia, which is projected to see 35 percent earnings growth, and thus has a PEG ratio of 1.0. Is twenty-five times forward earnings then "cheap" for Procter & Gamble? It would look so, certainly in comparison to Nvidia's earnings multiple. But P&G is a mature company in an industry that is hard to grow (the population doesn't increase by much, nor do aggregate appetites and needs for things like detergent or diapers). Not surprisingly, its earnings per share are seen to grow only 7 percent over the coming years, resulting in a PEG ratio of 3.4, a high number, both relative to Nvidia and in an absolute sense. P&G shares have returned 53 percent over the past five years through April 2025. That's half what the overall market has returned in that time frame, with the S&P 500 (a good representation of the overall stock market) up 110 percent. The price you pay for a stock, its valuation relative to earnings and growth rates, matters meaningfully to your returns. PEG ratios in the 1.0 to 2.0 range are what I look for in entering a new stock, especially if I think the company has better growth potential than is priced into that figure.

While that treatise on fundamental value investing may seem a little long, the truth is I have barely scratched the surface. But I don't want to miss the point that there are plenty of other ways to invest. Let's talk about some of those now. Just as the 86th Street crosstown bus may be the right way to get across Manhattan, for some people, momentum, growth, or speculative investing may work better.

Growth investing is marvelous when you get it right. A company growing its revenues at a breakneck pace with promise to turn those revenues into earnings can be a great investment. Often, however, it is growth first, profitability later. If those earnings expectations don't come through, or the growth rate falters, it can be quite a crowded and chaotic exit from the stock for many investors. Momentum investing can also be a very successful methodology. This style entails buying stocks that have exhibited strong recent price gains, on the expectation that the pattern is likely to continue in the future. It is a measure of a stock's popularity amongst the investment community. Both methods are less concerned with valuation methodologies. In some cases, particularly in momentum investing, basic fundamental business analysis is ignored. To some investors, stocks do not represent the fractional ownership of a company and its cash flows, but are just a random collection of letters put together to form ticker symbols. This mindset takes its ultimate form in speculative investing. Often referred to as the "greater fool" method of investing, speculative investing makes no pretense at all about fundamental analysis or valuation concerns. It is based on the idea that whatever price is paid to purchase the shares, there will be someone—the so-called greater fool—who will be willing to buy them at a later date for a higher price. Sentiment and emotion drive the investing decision. Analysis plays no role.

Clients whom I admire and respect will sometimes bring me a speculative investment idea. It may be a small-cap company with no earnings. In recent years, it has often been a cryptocurrency idea. My response to them is always the same and I share it with you now. There is nothing wrong with speculating. Some people have made a lot of money by speculating. A quick look at Bitcoin's price chart makes that point clear. There are legendary short-term traders for whom the feel of the market is instinctive. As much as I admire those successes, I will never try to emulate them, for one important, foundational reason. When a client entrusts me with the management of his investments, that is an incredible display of faith. Trust is, frankly, the currency of the land in the investment management industry. I will never buy a speculative investment and risk a client's trust. If I do, and the stock goes down, how will I explain it? That I licked my finger and put it in the wind to determine it was a good buy? I always want to have the power of fundamental analysis and disciplined valuation methodology in making investments. That way, if a stock goes down, I can cogently explain why I bought it in the first place and, more important, what we should do with it now. Quite often, the right decision is to buy more, if nothing has changed in the original investment thesis. The confidence to do so will not be there if the original purchase was made on a whim.

In clearly telling you how I like to invest, by no means do I intend to imply that my way is the best or that I never make mistakes. No way of investing is foolproof. In the case of fundamental, long-term investing, sometimes your investment thesis is just plain wrong. A good example of this is the case of CVS, the pharmacy-retail company that over the past several years has vertically integrated with acquisitions of health insurance company Aetna and several in-home healthcare service providers. The strategy seemed a good one: Combine all the consumer-facing services of healthcare under one corporate umbrella. The strategy included in-store medical clinics to diagnose and treat minor injuries and illnesses. The mergers were consummated with large debt issuances. When the federal government pulled back on reimbursement for the Medicare and Medicaid patients that CVS was insuring, it coincided with a meaningful increase in costs for insuring customers who had deferred procedures during the pandemic. Margins dropped precipitously. In the five years after purchasing Aetna, revenues increased by 45 percent but net income tumbled by 30 percent. That's a bad combination for any stock. CVS shares decreased by 40 percent during that time frame.

In the case of CVS, cutting my losses earlier would have been better. The decreased government payments, the increased patient utilization ratios, and the debt load all evolved over a long time. There's no point in using twenty-twenty hindsight to invest, and using the CVS example can actually lead you to make an equally pernicious mistake: giving up on a stock too early because it isn't working out for you. As I write, I am locked in an intellectual battle over the shares of Cleveland-Cliffs, an integrated steel manufacturer. Cleveland-Cliffs mines iron ore and buys scrap metal, using both as raw material to produce steel that goes into cars, buildings, infrastructure, and all sorts of manufactured products. As a commodity producer, Cleveland-Cliffs is the sort of company that I would normally stay away from. It is highly cyclical, exposed to changing political winds and economic trends, and at the mercy of many factors, such as fuel costs, that are beyond its control. Indeed, the company is currently battling depressed steel prices, varying tariff rules, Chinese dumping of below-cost steel on the global market, and questions about the health of the automobile industry, one of its biggest markets. The stock traded at ten dollars a share before the pandemic, slid to under five dollars during the COVID-induced economic shutdown, rebounded to thirty-four dollars in 2021, and has since slid back to ten dollars. Colleagues, clients, and especially my comrades on CNBC continue to ask me why I own the shares.

The simple answer is, of course, that I think they are grossly undervalued, and here's why. To start with, management is unique at Cleveland-Cliffs. The chief executive officer, Lourenco Goncalves, is visionary in many ways. He knows that to be successful, he must build bridges with disparate parties: unionized employees, customers, suppliers, shareholders, bankers, just to name a few. With some he uses a feather. With others, a sledgehammer. Knowing how to use which tool and when in interpersonal dynamics is a distinct skill. It is rare to find someone adept at many, and that is Mr. Goncalves.

It is because of these skills that he has managed to make acquisitions that have built a company with ten times the sales it had five years ago. Ten times! Under his leadership, the company recently bought a competing company, Stelco. Following on the track record of buying AK Steel and ArcelorMittal US in 2020, it is likely that there will be synergies well beyond the initial projections. The combined company will be the second-largest steel company in the United States and poised for much greater profits on the other side of this steel price down cycle than before.

In many merger cases, "synergies" is a word for firing employees. Not the case with Mr. Goncalves. He has created excellent relationships with his unions, so much so that the union at another company, the venerable US Steel, actively lobbied for Cleveland-Cliffs to buy the company instead of Japan-based Nippon Steel. Add to his resume strong leadership in protecting the environment through replacing coal-fired steel mills with hydrogen-powered ones, and you can see the multiple ways in which this is not just a dynamic but an incredibly unique leader, one who can make an ordinary steel company produce results that are anything but ordinary.

In my opinion, when the steel cycle turns back up, Cleveland-Cliffs will likely enjoy the 15 percent EBITDA (earnings before interest, taxes, depreciation, and amortization—an important measure of cash flow and a typical way of valuing a manufacturing company) that it enjoyed five years ago. But on a revenue base that is ten times larger. If that happens, the company will produce cash flow in one year equal to the current market cap of the company. That means the shares currently trade at a price well below intrinsic value, on that basis. Time will tell, but that sort of fundamental business analysis is what I enjoy doing.

All these stock stories that I just discussed with you are my way of saying that I know, as an investor, where I am going. I am a fundamental, long-term investor looking for a dollar's worth of value selling at fifty cents on the dollar today. I'm willing to be patient and diligent in letting my investment thesis play out. I want you to know where you are going, too! And not just in investing. Knowing where you are going in the workplace is important as well.

I mentioned in the introduction that I've made plenty of mistakes. I used the very true aphorism that good judgment comes from experience, and experience comes from bad judgment. It's taken me a long time to know where I am going when it comes to my work persona. There was a long time when I thought I was a business leader, destined to be a famous CEO. While I am a leader, I am not a CEO. I've seen and met amazing CEOs. I work for an incredible one now at Cerity Partners. Those CEOs know where they are going and they know they are CEOs. They think all day long about strategy, whom to hire to execute on strategy, the right capital structure, and how to allocate capital to profitable ventures. As a professional investor and client advisor, I am going somewhere else.

There was a time I was a naval officer. Wow, did I ever enjoy that! I still marvel at the privileges I was given as a twenty-four-year-old whisp of a man. Driving nuclear-powered fast-attack submarines. Leading, living with, and learning from collections of incredible sailors. There was a long time when I harbored fantasies of being "career" navy, striving to become an admiral and have an even greater impact on world peace. There is scarcely a day that I don't think back about it. Alas, it was not to be. I was commissioned in the Navy in 1990. And as the decade of the 90s and my career unfolded, the Cold War came to an end. There is no question as to the role the US Navy submarine service played in ending it, and I am proud of my very small part in it. With the demise of the Soviet Union, though, the US Navy's submarine force shrank, its raison d'être gone. I decided to rejoin civilian life.

It may surprise you to hear that I don't consider myself destined to be a great investor—a Warren Buffett or Peter Lynch. I think I'm a good investor, maybe even very good, but it is not my judgment to make. If anything, I am a disciplined investor, specifically in that I *invest*. I make purchases of companies, not random stock symbols. I value good management, solid business models, and moats to protect those businesses against competition.

I am all of those things just described, and not any one of them. I am a leader, a strategist, a communicator, and investor. But above all, I am a keeper of trust. A client once described me as "earnest." It was high praise. I think about that often. On television, I lead with my chin and wear my heart on my sleeve. Remaining true to my character as a believable, intelligent, earnest—and imperfect—human being, I believe, enhances the investing messages I am trying to get across.

As I mentioned, sometimes I take a little ribbing on air, particularly when one of my investments theses is taking a little longer to play out or seems out of favor with prevailing market commentary. People sometimes ask me why I put up with it, why I don't fight back. Again, you have to know where you are going. I am not adept at trash talk or put-downs. It is a foreign thought process for me. I try my best to see the truth in what people say and take the teasing as good-natured busting of chops. I'll admit that once in a while the things that are said to me seem mean-spirited or below the belt. I let those comments reflect on the person saying them, as a reflection of where they are going. It has nothing to do with my destination. In the end, I think people respect that my opinions are well thought out, that I am not deterred by the naysayers, and that I respond to hostility with decency, respect, and self-awareness. At least that is what I would like to think. That is definitely the destination in my mind!

I hope you, too, can find where you are going. It is not easy. It takes time and you make mistakes along the way. Sometimes you take the subway when you're supposed to take a cab. And vice versa. Those mistakes not only make you a better investor, they make you a better person, one of substance and depth. I write in Chapter 8 about exploration. Unabashed inquisitiveness can lead you to wonderfully undiscovered investments. It can lead you to powerfully enriching business relationships. But it can include plenty of wrong turns along the way. Don't ever be deterred by a mistake. Pick yourself up, dust yourself off, and get back in the saddle, better for the lesson you've learned.

Chapter 2

Know Who You Are

MANY PEOPLE RIDE THE subway. Few of them find it as intriguing as I do. It's something I've known about myself forever. As a boy, there was one Saturday when as I was setting out from our Manhattan apartment, and my dad asked me where I was going. "I'm going to spend the day riding the subway, Dad," I replied. "No, you're not," was his terse reply. Up in smoke was my carefully laid out plan to travel through as many subway stations as I could in a day. It was the late 1970s and the city was in financial peril. Maintenance deferred for a lack of funds meant that spray-painted graffiti was in some cases almost all that held subway cars together. And cost consciousness meant that the police presence in the subway system was both meager and disinterested. Crime ran rampant. Not the perfect setting for a cherubic boy to spend the day.

That anecdote may sound cute to some and insane to others. The subway is not for everyone. Many find its subterranean lairs claustrophobic, the sounds cacophonous, and the smells malodorous. The crowding can certainly cause unease, and the danger of criminal activity looms consciously. On the latter point, as I write this book, the New York City Subway system is undergoing a horrific crime wave. I've always stepped back and looked around me as trains enter the station. I recommend you do, too. It's just a wise thing to do, plain and simple. Taking this all into account, it is no wonder that some people prefer the bus or walking. Some of my friends take the subway with me to and from the New York Stock Exchange for our CNBC appearances; others only use taxis, regardless of their relative inconvenience. Heck, I know people who drive to work, even though they live in the city. Given the traffic and cost of parking, that makes no sense to me, but I do not judge. Everyone has to know who he is and what works for him.

However, none of its negative attributes deters me from my love affair with the subway system. There is no part of its infrastructure that doesn't capture my attention and imagination. I consider the reasons for certain track layouts to this day, even in stations that I've known for decades. Why, for instance, do both the Uptown and Downtown Express trains get served by a common island platform at the Penn Station–34th Street stop on the 7th Avenue IRT? It is one of only two stations constructed this way in the entire system. This unorthodox layout prevents easy transfers between the Local and Express trains, with the side-oriented Local platforms requiring a trip down a staircase, through a passageway, and up another staircase to access from Express trains.

The picture below shows the layout. Contrast it with the more traditional Express-Local track layout in which trains going in the same direction can easily be accessed across an island platform, seen in the Times Square layout one stop further north.

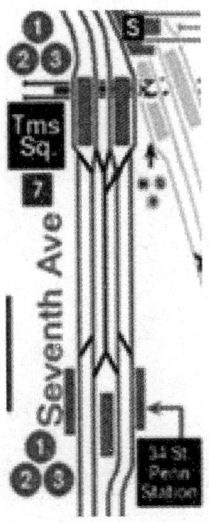

Map Credit: Peter Dougherty, Tracks of the
NYC Subway www.nyctrackbook.com

There is an answer, of course, and it is that in the early days of the subway, ridership from New Jersey and Long Island coming into Pennsylvania Railroad Station was projected to skyrocket. Having three available platforms, as opposed to the normal two, would alleviate the danger of crowding. The subway's designers knew that riders could easily change trains one station away at Times Square.

Beyond quirks, such as track layouts, the sublime creations manufactured to power and maintain the subway are a source of continual fascination. On W. 59th Street in Manhattan sits the original powerhouse for the first subway—the Interborough Rapid Transit Company (IRT) Powerhouse. Built in 1904 and pictured below, it is a monstrous but gorgeous edifice.

Photo Credit: Anitgng

Perhaps not as well-known as the iconic British Battersea Power Station that adorns Pink Floyd's famous *Animals* album cover, to me the 59th Street powerhouse is even more important and relevant. It was built by the renowned architecture firm of McKim, Mead & White (MM&W), the titan whose style defined New York's urban landscape at the beginning of the twentieth century. As with other MM&W edifices, such as the original Penn Station or the Manhattan Municipal Building, it relies on heavy stonework, prettified with flourishes, such as large arches, alternating masonry hues, and fancy palmettes and pilasters. It is imposing and engrossing at the same time.

Its beauty does not detract from its utility. Using coal delivered by barge from the Hudson River lapping at its western edge, the plant provided steam turbine–generated electricity to the subway system for its first fifty-five years. While its turbines have been obsolete for several decades, it still is a major source of steam, generated by its current owner, Con Edison, and piped throughout Manhattan for heating and cooling purposes.

Here's why I regale you with all this. Several months ago, a new client joined me. A very sophisticated woman, she lives not far from the 59th Street powerhouse. Upon hearing this, I exhorted almost involuntarily, "Oh, you are right near the steam plant." Having no idea what I was talking about, she looked at me as if I had three heads. Momentarily crestfallen and a little embarrassed, I moved on in the conversation. But the moment sticks with me.

In case you can't tell, I am a little bit of a dweeb. Depending on your reference, this can be defined as a boring, studious, or socially inept person. There are other, less flattering interpretations. I stuck the label on myself, but by no means am engaging in self-deprecation. I know who I am. I know what turns me on. I know where to look for creative inspiration. My muses are not the same as many other peoples, and that is absolutely okay. Science has noted the connections between people whose social skills may be less mainstream and affinities for rail-based transit. The uniformity of spinning wheels, the predictability of schedules, and the firm knowledge of where a trainline goes all appeal to those whose mastery of more amorphous social norms is not as well developed. Lest anyone take offense, I will be clear: I speak of myself only.

The point is, you have to know yourself. In all walks of your life. I know myself as someone for whom the subway system is a source of comfort. Others will find this anathema. I get that. However, by knowing yourself and not shying away from or hiding your true personality, you are apt to be your most effective. While I haven't brought it up with her since, I think that client liked my interjection about her proximity to my favorite power plant. There is sincerity and genuineness in being yourself in front of people. At any rate, I don't think I have it in me to be anyone else. As much as I may admire (or not admire) some of my co-contributors on CNBC, there's no way I could adapt any of their styles, unless it dovetails with my own. Nor would I want to.

The importance of knowing who you are and being true to yourself is absolutely vital in investing. In the previous chapter, I started to cover this notion by equating investment styles with knowing where you are going on the subway. Let's extend that discussion. As an investor, professional or otherwise, you will be flooded with information, opportunities, and pitches. If you don't know who you are, you are likely to set your course by the shiny objects that pass in front of you. This is dangerous. In investing, quite often flashiness can be a false lure.

I find myself often challenged by people with new ways to invest. These proponents breathlessly tell me they will make traditional equity investing obsolete. Alternative investments, AI-managed portfolios, social media–based investments, ESG (environmental, social, and governance). While some of what I just listed is absolutely viable, it can be very hard to separate the wheat from the chaff. This is especially true for the amateur investor. In fact, because a new investment pitch can be so seductively alluring, it can be diabolical in its power to attract new adherents, many of whom will regret getting involved.

Case in point: When the acute phase of the COVID-19 pandemic ended, and humanity began to live again, there were plenty of celebratory parties. At one such shindig, in the spring of 2021, there was music and food and dancing galore. It was a wonderful sight. Thrown by a client of mine, the party had many twenty-somethings in attendance, including one of the client's sons. During a break in the action, this young man—a very intelligent, well-spoken, handsome lad—careened over to where I was standing and thrust his phone in my face. "Do you see this?" he asked in a voice loud enough to be heard over the thumping music. It was a price chart of a cryptocurrency, Dogecoin, that had gone on an absolute tear over the past few months. The trajectory was basically straight up. The precise words of the conversation eluded me because of the pulsating rhythm, the gyrating lights, and the overall party atmosphere. But my young friend's position was clear: Why on earth would he bother with the dodgy old 10 percent-ish annual returns in the stock market, when he could make those kinds of returns in a day or two with cryptocurrency?

Now, we know how that story ends. Dogecoin was down 90 percent over the next year. There's no free-money tree from which you can pluck endless returns without risk. That's not how the world of investing works. And I can hear the words of the cryptocurrency acolytes now when they howl at me, "Yeah, but so what? Dogecoin is up almost ten-fold off that low. All you have to do is hold on." My perspective is that is absolutely correct. All you have to do is hold on (hold on for dear life, or "HODL" as the adherents say). The truth is, some will hold on, but by far, most will not. This is where it is important to know who you are. If you are not cut out to HODL, then stay away.

There are times in my investing life where I've got to hold on. There are times when anyone's investment style goes out of favor. If you know who you are, then you'll know why you've picked a particular stock to begin with. It will keep you in it, when the position is moving against you. Take Cisco Systems as an example.

Cisco Systems is one of the original pioneers of the internet. The switches and routers it develops are critical parts of the physical infrastructure on which modern digital communications rely, a fact going back to the internet version 1.0 in the 1990s. I've been invested in Cisco for about ten years. It bears pointing out that this is long after the infamous "Anyone

Wanna Buy a Bridge?" cover article from well-known business periodical *Barron's* in May 2000. Chronicling the company's Olympian ascent to the top of that era's stock market, that moment seemed to catalyze the end of the go-go 1990s tech and telecom boom, ushering in the recession and bear market of the earlier 2000s.

But my initial purchase was in the summer of 2015. I hope that some of you read that and say, "Wow, that is a long time ago." Precisely the point! If you can find a great company at a great price, like Cisco at that time, you buy it. And if you are right, it can go on performing for years and years. For taxable investors, the ability to defer capital gains tax by holding stocks over many years is tremendous. When I purchased it, it traded at a very reasonable multiple of 13x forward earnings and a 3 percent dividend yield. This was a far cry from the >100x multiple and no dividend that it traded at during the internet bubble. Oh, how the mighty are fallen!

I've been able to hold Cisco shares all these years, getting performance on par with the market overall, but with a heck of a lot less drama. Through the first eight years, Cisco's total return (share price plus dividends) exactly equaled that of the S&P 500. It's beta, however, has been less than 1.0 for most of that time. Beta is a measure of how much a company's stock price moves in response to moves of a similar direction in the market overall. In essence, it is a measure of volatility. So when I say I've had a lot less drama with Cisco, it is that beta measurement less than 1.0 of which I speak. But in the past three years, Cisco's share went through a swoon. And this is where the punchline comes in. Because I know who I am, because I am experienced in the exact life I've lived, I've known how to handle this swoon. I'm telling you this so you will be able to recognize your own innate talents.

Cisco's shares started declining in the summer of 2023. The normal cadence of customer orders had been seriously affected by the COVID-19 pandemic. At first during the pandemic, they dried up as the global economy shut down. Then, as recovery took hold in 2021, there were supply chain snafus. Both goods and people that Cisco needed to manufacture its products were held up. Remember all those ships parked outside Long Beach, California, waiting for a turn to unload? How about the Evergreen Group ship stuck sideways in the Suez Canal? Those incidents represented, both literally and figuratively, the issues Cisco and many other companies were facing. Cisco's customers responded by over-ordering, unsure of how much product they would get, but desperate to get as much as they could. In the end, supply chains unclogged and customers found themselves with far more Cisco products than they needed, as their larger-than-normal orders got filled. What happened next is a classic inventory adjustment: Orders plummeted, Cisco's guided earnings were below expectations, and the stock got hit. From August 2023 to August 2024, Cisco's share price declined by 20 percent, while the S&P 500 rose by 20 percent. Clients were upset and I had to answer not only to them, but also to the general public through CNBC appearances.

But an inventory adjustment is a temporary thing. It is not usually a fatal blow to a company, and it wasn't in Cisco's case. In the summer of 2024, Cisco reported the first of three consecutive quarterly earnings reports in which it both exceeded expectations and raised guidance. The experienced management team took advantage of its very strong balance sheet and cash flows to buy a company, Splunk, that catapulted both its cybersecurity and artificial intelligence applications, two high-growth sectors of the digital economy. Earnings conference calls with the professional analyst community made the point clear: The effects of the pandemic were behind them. Cisco was back on track. In early January 2025 its shares had returned 27 percent since that August 2024 low, while the S&P 500 returned 10 percent. I continue to hold Cisco shares and believe that for the next few years they are likely to give a better-than-average return.

A big mistake would have been to sell Cisco in the summer of 2024. I was certainly tempted to! It would have allayed the heat I was taking for holding it. But I knew myself. I knew the way I analyzed companies. I had lived through similar experiences in the past. While it wasn't comfortable to continue holding, I felt confident that it would turn out to be the right call.

While the Cisco story turned out well, not all of them have. A similar narrative happened with shares of Intel many years ago, and it had a decidedly worse outcome. While the inventory adjustment at Cisco did not change the long-term investment thesis, what happened at Intel did. Widely regarded as the pioneer in semiconductor manufacturing, in the mid-2010s Intel ran into significant problems. It struggled to maintain its lead building cutting-edge chips, ceding its position to more nimble companies like Nvidia and

Advanced Micro Devices. As a result, it struggled both to hire the best chip engineers and to acquire smaller companies that could enhance its capabilities. Both found its competitors more attractive enterprises to join. It lost key customers, such as Apple, and could not proceed with its developments in new sectors, such as mobile telephony. Its CEO position became a revolving door and strategic course changes ended up burning tremendous amounts of capital.

I purchased Intel originally in 2013 and it tripled over the next six years. Once all its problems became apparent in 2018, it started a multiyear decline. I ended up selling after seven years at twice my purchase price—a good, but not great, return. For much of the holding period, I felt similarly about Intel's long-term prospects as I do now about Cisco. But in Intel's early decline, I missed the secular change it was going through. I'm glad I sold when I did. The stock has been cut in half since. Truly a sad story.

I tell you the Intel story to make a point: Nobody gets it right all the time. *Nobody*—no matter how well you know yourself and your investing style. Humility is vital in investing. Anyone who says he never makes a mistake investing is one of those flashy objects I mentioned. Stay clear of them.

Knowing who you are, being confident in what you do, and carrying yourself with humility have deep applicability in the workplace. It takes time to develop as a business person. It's easy to feel uncertain and insecure, especially early in your career. As a young person, one doesn't have the experience and judgment on which to carefully consider options, and yet even the smallest of decisions can seem momentous given the long time horizons entailed. Negotiations with clients and colleagues are fraught with the peril of possibly being taken advantage of.

When I was a young man in the Navy and in my formative years in finance, at times I was untrue to myself. It took me a while to find out who I really was. Some of the role models I had growing up used methods that worked for them, but not for me. As I tried some of these on—including screaming rage, bombast, and not giving an inch in negotiation—I realized the hard way that these just did not work for me. Any victories I perceived were tainted by the dim feeling I had of having lost more in personal rapport than I had gained.

Sometimes the best lessons are the ones that are the most uncomfortable to learn. When I went to sea as an ensign aboard my first submarine, I was as green as any junior officer could be. I don't mean seasick green; I mean unripened. While by title, officers are in command over enlisted personnel, in practice it's a different matter altogether. I found this out one day in Maneuvering, the control center for the propulsion plant. As an officer-in-training, learning to run the reactor and steam plant as the Engineering Officer of the Watch (Under Instruction), I was tasty bait for the chop-busting that goes on amongst a crew. The watch team in Maneuvering consists of three very experienced petty officers. As the ribbing progressed, I decided I would establish my dominance by telling a first-class electrician's mate to shut up. Bad idea. His one-word response? "Okay."

A submarine is a small ship. Word quickly ricocheted from bow to stern of this foolish young officer, the "George Ensign" or lowest-ranking member of the wardroom, having told a very respected crewmember to stuff it. Before the watch was over, my punishment was clear. I would be given the silent treatment for the rest of the underway. The crew would make sure to acknowledge and follow any orders I gave, but that was it. No helpful feedback on what needed to be done or guidance when my orders were wrong. And the rest of the fellow officers made sure I got the lesson, too. On a submarine, there is no off time and there is no "home" apart from work. You are in close confines with your shipmates throughout a voyage. No one would speak to me. It was a long two weeks.

I wish I could tell you that I fully learned the lesson then, at age twenty-four. Regrettably, I had a few more instances in my twenties that taught me my personality simply isn't domineering. I am much more of a team and consensus builder. And where agreement can't be reached, I've learned to disagree amicably. This is, in fact, an art. It is one I wish more people practiced in our day and age where disagreements over politics, sports rivalries, and even investments can often resemble the intensity of holy wars.

A key to disagreeing well is making sure the other person feels heard. This is where truly knowing who you are matters. If you are as comfortable with the position you are taking in a discussion as, say, I've described my position in Cisco or in navigating unique subway stations, then you need not feel insecure when someone takes a countering view. You can really listen to a dissenting opinion and give it full consideration. Doing so doesn't lessen your argument. It simply engages your counterpart. By truly hearing what he is saying, you authenticate his position. Doing so does not, in any way, give ground on your own, different point of view. You may actually find out something about your position that you didn't know. Empathy is a tremendous asset.

At my stage of the game, I actually find it fun to kind of let up a bit in an argument. It's almost like the technique in a tug-of-war where instead of both sides pulling with all their might and getting nowhere, you suddenly give ground. The opposing team suddenly surges backwards and, having leaned into its position so hard, falls to the ground. The equivalent is to disarm your intellectual opponent by simply saying: I understand your position. That simple act of giving ground can be completely disarming. In turn, it can help your opponent better understand your position. In short, by not feeling you have to win every point, you're liable to be much more convincing and, in turn, win more of your confrontation.

So, consider this advice when next you find yourself attacked online, in social media, or in person. Really knowing who you are, and staying true to yourself, is your path to success. If you follow this path, you are likely to not only disagree well, but to be grateful for the interaction. Therein lies the art: finding reasons to be grateful when you least expect it. You can learn this the hard way, by signing up for the Navy, grinding through boot camp and nuclear training, and living for years on a submarine. Or, you can take a ride on the subway with me and learn it the easy way.

Chapter 3

Patience

ONE OF THE MOST formative experiences in my life was my seven years in the Navy. I continued to invest in stocks while serving as a submarine officer, and I had to make sure my investment choices would stand the test of time. The ship would pull away from the pier and the hatches would close, sometimes for months at a time. Under the waves, there was no internet with which to check stock prices or listen to the latest earnings call. It is during this time that my long-term investment time horizon was honed. That horizon depends on finding profitable companies with moats to competition and strong, experienced management teams with strategic vision. The price I paid for a share then, as now, had to represent good value in relation to current earnings and cash flows, the growth rate of both those metrics, the experience of the management team, and the risks inherent in the business models. In fact, it had to have a protective discount to the value I calculated from those metrics. After all, when I was at sea, it might be many weeks after a market-moving event before I would find out about it, let alone be able to trade on it. The long-term investor's mindset is that of a co-owner, not a trader. Stocks to us are not just random collections of letters strung together in ticker symbols. They represent fractional ownership in a company: its successes (profits), failures (losses), opportunities, risks, and rewards. This mindset gets away from trading stocks on the perceived quality of a quarter's earnings. It is the trader's mentality to care not a whit for the company's long-term strategy and to instead focus on the minutiae of moment-by-moment trading. This distinction of mindset is not to denigrate others' ways of participating in the stock market. As we will see in the next chapter, there are many ways to make money in the stock market. But this discussion is about the patience required to be an excellent long-term investor.

The subway has plenty of its own moments in which patience pays off. My earliest subway rides occurred in the 1970s, a time in which New York City almost went bankrupt. The municipal government's perilous finances provided very little money to maintain the subway infrastructure and it showed in many ways. Trains would break down—that is, the few that ran after drastic schedule reductions.

In 1979, I sang in a church choir after school at the Church of the Transfiguration—nicknamed the "Little Church Around the Corner"—a beautiful, courtyard-bounded church set back from the street in what is now called the NoMad (North of Madison Square Park) neighborhood of Manhattan. We practiced twice a week, and getting there from Trinity School on the Upper West Side required a sub-way ride on two lines: my well-known "home territory" of the 1, 2, and 3 IRT line, and the more foreign and mysteri-ous Broadway BMT line. On this line, even the designations were different—letters instead of numbers—and in weird combinations, too. The N, the RR, and the QB. What on earth were they meant to signify? The one thing this partic-ular line did not signify was timeliness. I remember waiting on the Times Square platform for what seemed an eternity, with the salsa sounds of Record Mart, the Latin music record store (a famous Times Square Station landmark) humming in the background. It left an indelible mark on me about the inept municipal governance at the time. However, the waiting eventually paid off. The train arrived and I got to the church. No harm done. But the memory of that long wait on the platform stuck with me.

Maybe it is from all that waiting in the subway that I learned patience. Today, the NYC Subway system runs effi-ciently, with a minimum of delays, but during my childhood there were plenty of inexplicable and long periods where a train would stop in the tunnel before moving on. Of course, if you know where you're going and what you're doing, you will get where you want to go eventually.

Patience is, to me, probably the greatest investing virtue. Often on CNCB, I am razzed by my co-contributors about how long I have held a stock. We tease each other a lot and it is mostly—mostly—in the good-natured manner of a sports team where everyone not only trusts each other, but believes in each other's innate talents. And the truth is, sometimes the teasing about my hold period is apt. Sometimes, you have to hold a stock a long time before its rewards are realized. These are times in which you are forced, especially in the public crucible of CNBC, to hone your investment thesis, to test its merits. If you are good at what you do, if as an analyst you are willing to do the deep-dive diligence on a stock, then that holding period can anneal and strengthen your conviction in the name. But, make no mistake, that diligence is work: You need to figure out what it is you need to know to make the investment call and then go get it. It might be perusing every word in every footnote of the annual report. Or, it may be calling the management team to discuss the company's strengths, weaknesses, opportunities, and threats (business school students will recognize this as the SWOT analytical structure). Frankly, one of the best indicators I have found is interviewing the suppliers of a company. They are often the first to see the up-and-down swings in the business cycle. In the stock market, the determination of an undervalued company comes down to seeing something important which the market overall is missing or dismissing.

Just because your investigation gives you the inspiration to determine that a particular company's stock is undervalued doesn't mean that it will instantly go up. The act of your buying shares does not immediately ring the bell that releases the intrinsic value racehorse from its starting gate. Again, patience is required. The nautical necessity that historically led me to this style of investing became practical as I transitioned from the Navy to being a professional investor. Now responsible for other people's money, as well as my own, I learned to detest losses. Bad enough as it is when it is your own capital, it becomes far worse when you have to answer a client's query about why you bought *that* stock at *that* price. The art of identifying stocks trading at a discount to their perceived intrinsic value became vital. This is the mantra of a value investor.

A case in point is my long-standing investment in shares of General Motors (GM). As I write this, GM is having a banner year, up 20 percent through the first quarter of 2024. But that excellent performance has been long in coming. For the past ten years, GM's annual return has been 5.8 percent, about half that of the S&P 500, the index most people use to track the stock market overall. Indeed, investing in GM has felt quite often like waiting for the Broadway BMT. But during the wait, I've made sure I know where I am going with the investment. By that I mean I've watched the company grow earnings-per-share 11.9 percent per annum during that time frame. Free cash flow—the amount of cash left over for shareholders to maintain and finance ongoing opera-tions—has tripled. That has enabled the company to pay down debt and increase dividends to shareholders. The fact that these key operating metrics—earnings per share and free cash flow—have increased at a more rapid rate than the share price has created a true windfall for shareholders: meaningful share buybacks. The company has used its excess cash to buy back its own shares on the open market to such a degree that the number of shares outstanding has shrunk by 40 percent over the past ten years. This means that for a given level of profitability, there are fewer shares of stock over which to spread the gains (see where that term "share" of stock comes from?). You can see how important this is when you consider that earnings per share have gone up almost twice as fast as net income since 2013. With fewer shares to spread the net income across, long-term shareholders have enjoyed a greater and greater portion just by being patient.

There's an interesting subtext to what I've just written. If net income has gone up by 6.6 percent per annum for ten years, and earnings per share have gone up by 11.9 percent, why is it that the share price has gone up by only 5.8 percent and what does that lag imply? The simple answer is that not a lot of people like GM. Some people have the twentieth-century perception of GM: It makes blah cars at best; it teeters on the brink of insolvency during recessions. It doesn't have the sex appeal of a modern-day social media, AI software, or cutting-edge semiconductor stock. That's okay. There's not a lot of sex appeal in riding the R train from 42nd Street to 23rd Street. But there is efficiency and success if your goal is to get to choir practice at the Little Church Around the Corner. And there is efficiency and success in owning shares of GM, if your goal is to be a business owner—albeit a fractional one—in an essential company, one that consistently grows its profit while providing a product people need and want.

Just a little more on this sentiment issue with regards to owning GM shares:

Over the past few years there's been a lot in the media about how the company is a bad investment, such as that electric vehicles are going to turn internal combustion engines into dinosaurs, that GM doesn't have the money or skills to compete with Tesla, that the labor unions have eaten the car companies' lunches, that the Chinese are coming with ultra-low-cost cars and will kill all Western car companies, and so on. As a participant in the media, I can say that the media's business model is not to tell you good news—that doesn't get eyeballs on the tube and advertising dollars in the door. The media want to stoke fear and controversy because that's what gets you to turn on the newscast or to click on the news website.

As a case in point, when the United Auto Workers recently won a five-year contract with GM, the news reports were replete with how the company got fleeced, how it would never be able to compete with non-unionized and foreign competitors, how this was a death knell for legacy automakers. It's a good thing nobody told GM's management. A couple of months after the contract was finalized, GM announced revised forward earnings guidance that projected significantly improved earnings going forward. The increased cost of the new contract would be offset by cost cuts elsewhere in the business. About fifteen minutes' worth of analyzing GM's recent financial statements would have revealed that about a 2 percent average selling price increase in GM cars over the coming five years would entirely offset the increased labor costs. Add in the additional cost cuts, and the company looks like an earnings juggernaut. Again, you wouldn't know it if you listened to the media. I do my best in my CNBC appearances to state the objective truth, as I see it, regardless of whether it is salacious or boring.

My point is not to laud GM, nor to lambast the media, to which I contribute and from which I benefit. Who knows? By the time this book goes to print maybe I will have sold off the stock. It is to emphasize the importance of patience. Knowing what you are doing, how you are investing, and where you are going is vital to staying on that platform when it feels like the train will never come. Knowing what you're doing in the case of investing means knowing your investment style. Mine is a deep analytical style. I don't rely on others to do the research. I do it myself. It involves carefully studying financial statements, evaluating management skills, assessing business risks and opportunities, and determining the price I want to pay for the shares. If I do these things diligently, then I know which platform of which train line I am on. I may not know the exact time the train will come, but I know it will come and it will get me where I want to go.

The importance of patience applies strongly in the workplace. Any business that is building, growing, and succeeding will have its share of aggressive, opinionated strong personalities. Not all are going to vibe with your way of thinking, your way of investing, your way of doing. I have always felt that the two worst things you can do in a disagreement are to either let it become a full-on fight or to meekly acquiesce to the other person's point of view, only to stew on it in your internal dialogue for days and weeks afterwards.

I carry memories with me from the Maneuvering Room of a nuclear-powered attack submarine, from the set of CNBC's *Halftime Report*, from boardrooms, client meetings, and one-on-ones with colleagues where the fuel is always there for a full-on confrontation. All those venues are full of opinionated alpha types, strong-willed and not likely to easily be convinced of new viewpoints. In my younger days, I acted badly by riling up my opponent, sometimes starting the whole mess myself. To me now, doing so is like losing one's patience when you know the subway will come down the tunnel, if you simply wait. All you need is to do your homework so that you know you are right. If you've done that, then you don't need to do anything other than wait for the truth to win the day.

Sometimes I have been ridiculed about my investments on live TV or questioned during professional settings in manners that I have found highly offensive. It is one thing to challenge a business person's assumptions or analysis. It is another thing to disrespect an experienced, accomplished human being publicly. The first way can be helpful for elucidating the full truth of a situation. The second simply makes the accuser look bad. I often feel both offended and, oddly, guilty when attacked intellectually. Mind you, I mean something different than being disagreed with. I mean put-down, humiliated. The offense is, of course, natural to feel. The guilt and embarrassment, though, are odd to write about. It is a feeling as if to say, "Hey, maybe this person's right. Maybe I am a dummy and maybe I deserve the ridicule."

Here's a case in point. A few years back, I was asked by my firm's CEO to test out a new investment strategy. This is a good opportunity to point out that I am blessed, and I do mean blessed, to work at a fabulous firm. I feel strongly that Cerity Partners is the best collection of experienced, intelligent, and tremendously decent advisors, all pulling their oars in the same direction: to take care of our clients' needs and be the best at what we do. The esprit de corps and warm camaraderie with my colleagues are things I've not found in any other firm. So, I was surprised at the reception when I presented the new strategy to the firm's Investment Committee.

The surprise was not that there was disagreement about the strategy. What I proposed was new and unlike anything the firm had done to that point. It would have been a bad sign had there been no pushback, no dissension. The manner in which the discussion progressed surprised me in its intensity, though. There were some whose comments clearly displayed not just disagreement, but harsh judgment about the trading strategy. This included its methodology but notably, the clear message that I was putting the firm at legal and reputational risk. The meeting became difficult for me, with a meaningful faction almost up in arms, not just against my proposal but also against the quieter members of the group for not criticizing my ideas in the same harsh terms. After the meeting, several people came up to me and said they had never seen such a contentious meeting.

I was taken aback. Going back to that guilty sensation, I wondered if indeed I was risking the firm's reputation. With a little introspection, I realized that my overall style of investing, picking individual stocks, sat ill with some of my colleagues, as it worked at cross-purposes with their marketing pitch to clients that our firm's objectivity was centered on the fact that it had no internal stock pickers. The advisors focused on risk management and asset allocation, while outsourcing the specific investment selection to third-party investment managers. This is a common wealth management practice and completely different from my methodology. But the die was now cast. A group of people within the firm had publicly announced they were my adversary. Here's where the patience of waiting for the subway kicked in. Going head-to-head with any of them, either in the presentation or in its immediate aftermath, would never have worked. So, I waited. And in the years—yes, years—that followed, my firm added more and more people doing exactly the type of investing that I do: selecting individual securities. The business was profitable. It was also populated by dozens of people—professional, good, and kind people—on par with the excellence of those colleagues for whom my strategy was anathema. The effect was to blunt any further criticism. My group took exquisite care of our clients, we were fun to be around, and we got along with our colleagues. The intensity of the disagreement faded with the passage of time. An occasional uncomfortable moment occurred with my opponents, but their bite was blunted by patiently allowing the success of my group and strategy to show itself.

This vignette is neither a vent nor a payback. It is true and accurately describes my point. I've never been a knife-fighter. I've preferred to rely on intellect and hard work in the form of diligent research. Many times, I had to wait for success. Just like waiting for the Broadway BMT Local to take me to choir practice.

The opposite of being patient in the stock market is rapid trading in and out. There is a documented inverse correlation between the number of trades an average investor makes and the investment returns. The intersection of zero-commission trading and high-bandwidth internet has allowed the proliferation of online brokerages. Many of these websites promote the "democratization" of trading. They cloak themselves in the noble mantle of "being for the little guy." I've read the Securities and Exchange Commission (SEC) disclosure documents for these firms. In the "Risk Factors" section you can peruse what might happen to them if military conflict breaks out, if severe weather occurs, if interest rates spike—you name it. But nowhere in the disclosures do they suggest what might happen if their customers wise up.

An informed investor realizes that buy-and-hold is the best strategy. Consider the following chart:

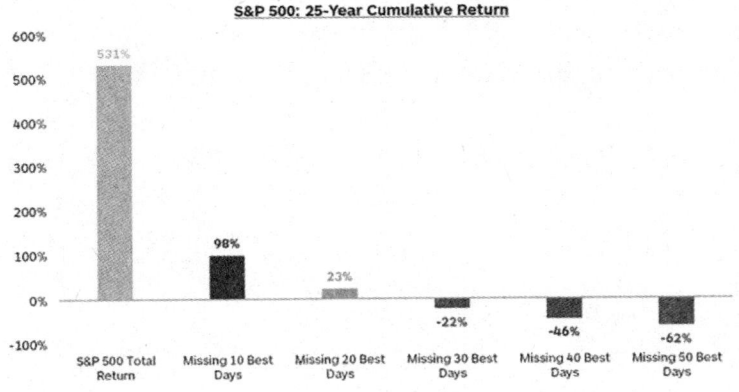

Source: Jim Lebenthal

I use this chart in client discussions often. It shows the folly of trying to be nimble in timing the markets. In short, it tells us that simply buying the overall stock market (represented in the left-most column by the S&P 500) and holding it over long periods of time is the recipe for success: Over twenty-five years, $1,000 becomes $6,310 by doing nothing but staying in the market. If, however, you try to time the markets and inadvertently miss some of the best market-return days, your overall return goes down quickly. For example, in the third column from the left, if you miss less than one best day per year on average, the original $1,000 investment becomes $1,230—far less than the damage done by inflation in a quarter-century and far less than simply buying-and-holding the stock market overall.

Ironically, it's easy to get out of the market when you try to time it. When the gains have been abnormally high, above the long-term average, many people say they want to take their money out of the market and wait for a good opportunity, presumably much lower, to get back in. Often they have distinct catalysts in their minds for why to do so now:

"The Fed's going to raise rates."

"This president is a disaster for the country."

"Country X is going to invade Country Y."

Or, my personal favorite:

"I've just got a feeling."

The hard part, however, is knowing when to get back in. Those best days referred to in the chart? They tend to come very close on the heels of the worst days in the market. That means to get back in, an investor has to buy when it feels absolutely like the worst time to do so, when the market has been clobbered. I can tell you from my experience with thousands of investors over the years that very few can do that.

Sometimes, the retort I hear to the chart is, "Yeah, but what about missing the worst days?" Well, by definition, the returns would be higher. But, if you haven't agreed with me on the point thus far, consider in different terms what you are potentially giving up. The 531 percent total return is 7.6 percent per annum. Sure, you can go for higher, but is 7.6 percent not enough? I ask myself this when, again, someone—usually on social media—lays into me for how long I've owned GM or Cisco Systems or Citigroup. These are companies that, over decades, track the return of the market overall. Yes, they have lagging periods, but then they make up for them over time. When people turn their noses up at them, I wonder if they've become a little bit jaded by whatever stock du jour has had a marvelous run. It's the wrong comparison to make. If you've earned your wealth through hard work, you should want to grow and protect it, knowing that buy-and-hold will get you through the good and the bad times. All it takes is patience.

Patience is a virtue. It's good to remember that before you switch to the Local track, thinking that the Express will never show, or when you're about to give up on that stock that you've done such great research on but hasn't budged, or when you feel your business efforts are going nowhere. Quite often, patience is the greatest virtue.

Chapter 4
Discipline

———————————

IT WAS A MORNING in late 2001. I was on the subway, making my way to work in the Financial District of Downtown Manhattan. The normal meditation of thinking through the coming day's events, imagining the lives of my fellow travelers, and general calm of being in the subway enveloped me when, suddenly, the subway car was flooded with sunlight. The realization hit before the thought coalesced in my head: I was on the wrong train. The warmth of the light mitigated my bewilderment, but only slightly. I was on the Manhattan Bridge bound for Brooklyn. I would certainly be late for work and would have to figure out my way back across the East River.

The impact of 9/11 on the subway system was major. Steel beams plummeting down from the World Trade Center had pierced street surfaces, stabbing into the subterranean tracks. Shown below is a well-known picture of the damage to the Cortlandt Street Station of the 1 line.

Photo Credit: George Miller NYCTA

During the long rescue and recovery operations at the World Trade Center site, much of the Downtown subway service was discontinued or rerouted. As befitted my long-time love affair with the NYC underground maze, I knew that the Broadway Express (N/R if you're interested in the details) would get me close enough to One New York Plaza, my Goldman Sachs office building, and that I could easily transfer to it from my home line, the 7th Avenue IRT at Times Square. What I didn't realize was that occasionally service on the Broadway Express would take a hard left at Canal Street to head east to Brooklyn via the above-ground tracks on the Manhattan Bridge.

Of course, I eventually made my way back to Manhattan. But that feeling of newness, of discomfort twinged with excitement at the experience of something new—sunlight on my quotidian underground travel—stays with me to this day. We should always be looking for new experiences. The serendipity of the unexpected can widen the field of vision for our outlook in life. This is true in life, in investing, and in business. I write this while simultaneously hearing the investing advice of my father: "Stick to your knitting, Jim." Indeed, there is a balance to be struck between gaining professional expertise in repeating the processes that make you successful and making sure you don't stagnate by never trying something new. Flit about like a gadfly and you're unlikely to be a success. But only do one thing and your brain will ossify.

This concept of serendipity taking hold and leading to new experiences has often happened to me on the subway. It is so important in my life that Chapter 9 is fully devoted to it. As a preteen, I remember taking the subway with my mother down to the South Ferry Station to meet my father. Somehow, we ended up on the inner loop platform at the old station. This was where the seldom-used and soon-to-be-discontinued Bowling Green Shuttle would connect the east- and west-side lines of the IRT. Not only was it not where we wanted to be, but it was also a little dangerous with oversized gaps between the train doors and the sharp-radius curve of the platform. While excited to experience a new location in the subway, the discovery was offset by my mother's irritation and the station's inherent danger.

This concept of intellectual balance is expressed often in investing. In previous chapters, I advised you to know who you are and where you are going. The direct correlation to investing was to pick your investment philosophy. In my case, that is long-term fundamentals-based value invest-ing. Occasionally, I will experiment with a different type of investing, but only in limited and controlled circumstances.

An example is the dalliance I had with shares of Roku, the streaming TV company, from 2017 to 2019. The stock came to my attention one day while I was on CNBC. A noted short-seller (the name will not be shared so as to pro-tect all involved) came on the show and brutally excoriated a sell-side analyst who had just put out a bullish note on the name. Until that point, I could not have cared less about Roku. But the vehemence with which this investor attacked was a huge signal to me. I have found, more often than not, a direct inverse correlation between the emotion with which people promote their investment opinion and their actual knowledge of the same. I had to investigate what was going on with Roku.

What I found was a company growing revenues at hyper speed. The company was the sixth start-up ("Roku" is the Japanese word for "six") of serial entrepreneur Anthony Wood. There were no earnings at that time, nor projected in the immediate future, but the buzz about the company's ability to revolutionize streaming for TV was immense. This was a typical growth company. The momentum in the name was spectacular, bridging the two disciplines—growth and momentum—that often go hand in hand. So, I decided to participate in the fun. Bear in mind, this was pretty differ-ent from the cash-flow analysis that is the bread and butter of my trade. But boy, was it fun! Roku shares would sense-lessly go up almost every day. Any provocation would be the cause for more levitation: earnings reports, CEO interviews, news from competitors. It was all fuel for a torrid rise. Until it stopped. For no reason, the momentum just stopped. I decided to not press my luck and headed for the hills, selling for nice short-term gain. Interestingly enough, after a bit of a fall, the shares resumed their ascent and I participated again. As with the first go-round, I waited until the momentum stopped and then got off the train.

While it was fun to make money in this seemingly easy fashion, something left me uneasy about it. This just wasn't the way I was wired to make money in the stock market. Something in my DNA drives me to look for a dollar's worth of intrinsic value in a company's shares while they trade at a significant discount to that value in the public stock market (revisit Chapter 1 for more). In the same way that I could enjoy the sunlight hitting my face on that late fall morning subway ride, I could enjoy riding the momentum wave of a Roku run. But that subway was going in the wrong direction to get to work, and suddenly abandoning a lifetime of fundamental equity analysis to become, in effect, a day trader, would equally be moving in the wrong direction.

Oftentimes I see investors, sometimes my fellow CNBC contributors, changing their investment stripes at a moment's notice. One day they're a technical investor analyzing the charts, the next day a cryptocurrency maniac talking about Bitcoin "halvings," only to change stripes again the next day and become a "meme stock" investor, trying to imitate Roaring Kitty and his GameStop mania. My favorite moment is when such gadflies lecture me about why one of my fundamental picks is wrong by their lights.

A jack of all trades is a master of none. It is good to maintain a dose of humility in investing. This idea that we can be knowers of all things before they happen is truly a fool's errand. I found it amusing, for example, after Russia's invasion of Ukraine in 2022, that fellow portfolio managers became nuclear warfare experts overnight. Having spent time tracking Soviet ballistic missile submarines as an Officer of the Deck aboard US Navy submarines, I had a thought or two on the subject and I found my colleagues' suddenly acquired expertise dilettantish.

I will stick with my method of investing through its ups and downs. Every investment style can have moments of great success and miserable failure. But just as a restaurant shouldn't change its cuisine every night of the week, one should not flit about from one style to the next. Doing that will only ensure that you never accumulate enough experience in any one discipline to master it.

These thoughts are so, so true in the workplace.

Within the finance industry, I have served as chief executive officer, chief investment officer, chief financial officer, investment manager, and financial advisor, amongst other roles. Thankfully, and obviously, I have not served in all those roles simultaneously. I list them not to brag about my resume but to form a basis upon which to state: You have to know a lot of things to succeed in business. First and foremost is strategy. The business opportunities you pursue have to balance reward with risk. Both must be analyzed, quantified, and balanced. You have to know the law—not just by statute but by practical impact. One has to understand financing: Whether to use debt or equity in starting up a company and whether to allow employee capital contributions for the same are examples. And not least, the concept of leadership is beyond vital. While ambiguously conceptual in nature, leadership can partially be decomposed into central tenets such as selflessness, responsibility, intelligence, empathy, and faith, attributes which, when observed in a leader, are inspired in those being led. Charisma is contained in leadership. Self-sacrifice is its sine qua non.

That list of requirements to succeed in business is, of course, not comprehensive. Perhaps, then, it can be further filled out by what is not conducive to business success. Arrogance, conceit, closed-mindedness, and laziness are at the top of that list. If you have ever experienced a leader espousing these character traits, as I have, then you will know they are a recipe for failure. They are the hallmarks of entitlements. Success in a capitalistic society is not based on the party affiliation of a communist system or the hereditary nature of a monarchy. No one is intrinsically owed anything in capitalism. And while capitalism sometimes get knocked, it beats all the other systems. If you don't believe me, try living in socialist Cuba or read history books about the breadlines in Soviet-era Moscow.

You may be wondering about the tie-in to my opening anecdote of the subway ride that went amiss. As I remarked earlier: Good judgment is the result of experience, and experience the result of bad judgment.

Variously attributed to Mark Twain—as most good non-investment quips are, the financial ones usually being assigned rightly or wrongly to Warren Buffett—it captures the tone of balance that I am trying to strike in this chapter. Mistakes will be made. On your subway ride, in investing, and in business. It is vital that mistakes be made, so that lessons can be learned. Explaining away a wrong turn, acting as if it didn't happen, or blaming it on villainous entities negates the lesson. When the subway goes in a different direction than you thought it would, open your field of vision and take in the new surroundings. Don't live in the new surroundings; you have to get to where you were originally going. But take in the senses of the new. Learn the new experience. And then get back to what you are supposed to be doing, only now more informed, more experienced, and better equipped to make the right judgment calls. If I want to go across the Manhattan Bridge by subway, I know how to do it. At the same time, I know how to get to work efficiently.

Chapter 5

Investigate

FOR ME, THE NEW York City Subway system inspires bound-less curiosity. It comprises 472 stations spread over 248 route miles. Twenty-eight different routes are serviced by 6,553 subway cars. Twenty-four different storage yards are spread across the five boroughs of the city, ranging from the massive seventy-four-acre Coney Island complex to the rather cute five-track 137th Street Yard beneath Manhattan's Broadway. While simply lists to some, each of those data points sets my mind racing to understand why they exist, what purpose they serve.

Many fail to see the subway system's intricacies. Once my initial fascination set in, I satisfied it in countless ways. I studied not only the subway map, but the historical rendi-tions of it. This showed me where previous line routes had been placed, which further made me think about why they had changed. The best example of this is the two primary IRT (Interborough Rapid Transit) company lines in Manhattan:

the 1-2-3 going up the West Side, and the 4-5-6 on the East Side. These routes derived from the first subway line ever in Manhattan. Created in 1904, this line came north from City Hall on the East Side before turning ninety degrees at Grand Central Terminal to head west on 42nd Street. When it got to Times Square it turned back in its original direction to head up the West Side. That seemed like a good start for a rapidly growing city's mass transit system, and indeed it was. Within nine years of opening, the subway's popularity became quickly apparent, so the city contracted to sever the original line into three components. The path along 42nd Street was separated out into what is now the Times Square–Grand Central Shuttle. The two thus disembodied portions were extended: south from Times Square on the West Side and north along Lexington Avenue on the East Side. The resulting H-shaped route structure allows efficient, rapid transit from the primary residential areas of the upper half of the island to the main work districts of Midtown and Downtown, with a convenient crosstown connector.

Here's another interesting fact: The NYC Subway system crosses the city's major rivers (Harlem and East Rivers) fourteen times. Three of these are bridge crossings shared with passenger cars. The other eleven are tunnels. When the Holland Tunnel under the Hudson River was opened to vehicular traffic in 1927, the moment was so important that President Calvin Coolidge did the ceremonial honors. About 90,000 cars use that tunnel daily and have the privilege of paying seventeen dollars to do so. The Montague Street Tunnel for the subway system, on the other hand, had no fanfare for its inauguration, despite being of comparable length and being completed seven years earlier. Used by the BMT (Brooklyn–Manhattan Transit) company's Broadway and Nassau Street Lines, more than 30,000 passengers used this tunnel daily before the COVID-19 pandemic. These submarine crossings are mostly unremarkable to the travelers, which befits the fact that they are gratis with a $2.90 subway fare. The Montague Street Tunnel is just one of those eleven tunnels. That large a number created many opportunities to explore novel construction techniques. Some tunnels were bored under the muddy riverbed. Others were fabricated on land, sunk in the water, and then drained to create an airtight crossing. Some were lined with concrete, others with cast-iron collars. Most are well over a hundred years old and vital to the transportation system of the largest city in the nation.

These two examples of how the subway system was built are but a few of an endless list. It's not great party talk, I'll admit, to discourse on cut-and-cover construction vs. open-cut trackage. But when you start to consider their idiosyncratic advantages, one wonders if the open-air rights-of-way (elevated tracks, surface tracks, bridge crossings) are designed to inspire workers with the Oz-like vision of NYC on the fast-approaching horizon. Subways are all about maximizing worker efficiency. Perhaps the system's designers planned to do so by raising passengers' excitement level on the way in? And why do some subway cars have three doors on each side, while others have four? Lest you roll your eyes at seemingly nauseating trivia, there is a point here. The answer is that, before subways were a municipal convenience, they were private enterprises, run for profit. Private corporations built two original subway networks and operated them for profit for three decades. The city then built its own municipal network. Have you wondered why I insist on pointing out the full names of the subway networks—Interborough Rapid Transit (IRT), Brooklyn–Manhattan Transit (BMT), Independent (IND)? It's to press the point that innovation most often comes from commercial pursuit of profit. And sometimes that commercial profit goes too far. NYC did not need three independent networks at the time they were built. The two private companies went bankrupt and the city, recognizing the importance of what they had built, assimilated them into the municipal management of infrastructure. Now branded an essential service and backed by lower-cost, tax-free municipal debt, the perpetual NYC Subway was created.

With understanding of the construction, operation, and provenance of the subway, connections to investing are easy to make. In the first decades of the twentieth century, the subway represented the economic theory of creative destruction. Companies throughout the city had access to a quantum increase in workers, now released from the immediate confines of residential neighborhoods. This municipal cardiovascular system expanded city boundaries, creating new communities from previously inaccessible raw land. One can easily make the mental leap to the twenty-first-century equivalent of digital technology with not only its enhancement of existing technology, such as media recording, but also the creation from whole cloth of new applications, such as online commerce.

And let's take the concept down a few levels from the big-picture perspective. Understanding how things work is vital in investing. Case in point: share buybacks. In Chapter 3 ("Patience"), I touched on the importance of a company repurchasing its shares. With its conceptual importance in hand, let's get into the mechanics of how this is actually done. Successful companies across all industries engage in share repurchases. The range includes the largest companies in the world, such as Apple, to companies one-thirtieth that size, such as Citigroup.

I use those two examples because in both cases, the share buybacks result in meaningful reductions to the number of shares outstanding. In the ten years ended September 30, 2024, Apple's diluted outstanding share count decreased from 24.5 billion to 15.4 billion. That is a 37 percent reduction, or 4.5 percent annually on average. Similarly and coincidentally, Citigroup decreased its share count during that time period by the same 37 percent. By the standards of buybacks, those are meaningful decreases and can only be sustained over such a long period by companies that are operationally performing excellently. By contrast, you can't buy back shares over ten years by issuing debt to fund the purchases. A company can try that route for a short period of time, but eventually credit markets say "enough" and turn off access to credit not being used to build new businesses or expand existing ones.

But, just as with the subway, you have to dig deeper to get the details. Whenever I speak of share repurchases, I use a measure called "diluted shares outstanding." This is the most comprehensive measure of the number of shares across which net income must be spread. It includes convertible bonds that may be paid back in the form of newly issued shares and employee stock compensation that can also increase the share count. Simply relying on the "basic shares outstanding" will not capture the full economic picture. This is incredibly important! Companies routinely announce newly authorized share buyback programs. Annual reports and quarterly SEC filings (forms 10-K and 10-Q) will list the number of shares purchased at what price during reporting periods. But for many companies, these share prices do nothing more than compensate for the shares they have issued to employees as compensation (such as stock options and restricted stock awards) during the same period. This means the share count does not go down, and the earning-per-share figure does not improve. Only the diluted share count will tell you what the real impact of share repurchases is.

One further note: When a company reports earnings per share, accounting rules dictate that it uses the *average* share count over the time period in question. The income statement can thus be distorted by the reporting period time length, the number of shares issued, and the number repurchased. The gold standard is the diluted share count as reported on a company's balance sheet and statement of equity.

Share buybacks are but one small facet of investing. To me they are very important, even sacrosanct, as they represent an actual return of the money I have invested in a company. It is for that reason that the recently instituted excise tax in the 2022 Inflation Reduction Act on share buybacks rankles me so. I invested after-tax dollars in a company, so it's already been taxed. There's no justification for taxing a company when it gives me my after-tax dollars back by buying its own shares. And the idea that this tax will remain at 1 percent is unlikely. The camel's nose is under the tent, with the rest of its body soon to follow. Indeed, both political parties have proposed increasing this tax recently, to balance the federal budget.

To say that any aspect of investing is important requires knowledge of how it works. Just as the intricacies of block signaling (discussed in the next chapter) or the detail of the Montague Street Tunnel can enhance the way you ride the subway, so too are the minutiae of investing vital to being the best investor you can be. And it applies in general business as well.

Cerity Partners is the most dynamic firm I've ever been associated with. When I joined eight years ago, it had eighty people, managing about $9 billion in client assets. As I write now, we are over 1,300 people and with our affiliates have over $130 billion in assets under management. We've managed to grow by bringing in not just incredibly talented people, but exceedingly decent individuals, the sort you enjoy every interaction with. This includes disagreements, in fact, almost especially disagreement. There is an art to disagreeing. Done well, both participants understand and empathize with each other. It is the process by which we add to our depth of knowledge.

In a firm our size, role specialization is an absolute necessity. Specialization starts with departmentalization: investment advice, wealth management, legal, finance, and so on. Then, it goes deeper. Within our investment office we have strategists on equities vs. bonds, specialists in private markets vs. public, advisors focused on individuals and others focused on foundations and endowments. Here, though, is the real point to be made: If you want to be successful in business, you have to have an innate curiosity about all the areas your firm covers. You may be a specialist in one—as I am with public equities—but your ability to network, learn, and generate synergies from your colleagues will only come by being fascinated by what they do.

I sometimes relate this concept to people from my time in the Navy aboard submarines. A nuclear-powered fast-attack submarine is an almost incomprehensibly complex machine. The physics of the fission-powered nuclear reactors that drive these ships are based on the reality-altering concept that the atom can be split and, by so doing, matter can be converted into energy. Beyond that essential heart of the ship, networks of steam, high-pressure hydraulics, compressed gas, and electricity all enmesh in an engineering ballet. From this array of distributed power all the ship's functions come to life: steering and diving, internal atmospheric control, sensors and computers, weapons delivery. Trust me, that is a very incomplete list, but the point stands: The intricacy of a submarine defies description. I'll do my best to relive the experience for you here.

That experience included working with 130 other officers, chiefs, and crewmen to complete the ship's missions. Some of those were mechanics, some electricians, and some were cooks ("Mess Specialists" to be exact; like any military service, the Navy has its own language). A typical submarine has about fifteen different "ratings" or areas of expertise assigned to her. In order to qualify as a submariner, and wear the coveted "dolphins" insignia, you had to understand how all the systems and procedures of a submarine worked. In essence, you had to "turn every valve," that is, know what every component on the ship does and when to use it. You had to practice every casualty procedure (fire, flooding, radio-logical leak) until it was so ingrained in your memory that the steps became instinctive and you could do them without thinking. As an officer, particularly, you had to be prepared to lead any submarine evolution, be it shooting a torpedo, starting up the reactor, or fighting a fire on board. Every one of these events required coordination of many watchstanders. At any point in time, there are typically twenty to twenty-five men on watch in a submarine, with many more during com-plicated maneuvers or battle stations. There simply is no way to lead these situations unless you have the full understand-ing of every watchstation, its responsibilities, and the exact processes by which they are completed.

Submarine Service Insignia. Photo Credit: Jim Lebenthal

Now, I realize fully that not everyone can go aboard a submarine to live that experience. But there are other ways to grasp what I am speaking about. Here's an exercise I do. It's a little dorky (in case you haven't figured it out yet, that's me!).

Often when you land at the airport, you have to drive a good way to get into whichever city you're visiting. On those drives, take a look at the office buildings along the way. Highways to the airport are often major commercial areas. Often, these are the suburban outpost buildings of brand-name companies. Look at the names posted atop the buildings and ask yourself what goes on there and why they are located there. Are these provincial accounting departments, regional sales headquarters, or something else?

Here's an example. Planes normally land at Los Angeles International Airport from the east, and if you're on the left side of the plane you can see a cluster of low-rise office buildings just before the airport starts. Several aerospace company logos are visible including, prominently, Boeing. At first glance, this makes sense. LAX is a major airport and Boeing is a major manufacturer of commercial airlines. But think it through a little more deeply. Boeing is headquartered in Arlington, Virginia, for its proximity to Washington, DC, where regulatory decisions about commercial aviation and budget decisions for defense aviation are made. Boeing has major manufacturing operations in the Puget Sound region of Washington state and Charleston, South Carolina. With neither major factories nor headquarters in Los Angeles, what does Boeing do at this satellite location?

If you already know the answer, you'll have spotted the pun in how I phrased that question. In the twentieth century, Los Angeles became a major commercial locus for companies involved in the exploration of space. The Space Shuttle and other rocket-powered or similarly advanced space planes, such as the X-15 and SR-71, were conceived in LA. The El Segundo complex we are discussing is where Boeing assembles satellites for government and commercial use.

I am hoping that you will look for and explore (on the internet, that is) similar buildings on your travels. There is a plethora of biotech laboratories in South San Francisco just north of San Francisco International Airport. Your imagination can run wild at the outposts along the way into Chicago's O'Hare International Airport, marvelously served by Chicago's subway system. And don't even get me started about the data centers surrounding DC's Dulles International Airport. It defies belief and conjures up images of Machine City from the four *Matrix* films.

We know what goes on at massive headquarters like the new JPMorgan Tower in New York, which looms over an ever-rising NYC skyline like the Emperor's Tower rises over the Death Star in *Star Wars*. The same goes for the Salesforce Tower in San Francisco or the Comcast Building in Philadelphia, both the tallest in their respective cities. Those are nuclear reactors of activity: the heart and soul of a company. But wondering about and imagining the purpose of corporate outposts? It's like wondering if the balloon track in a subway yard would ever get used to turn around a train. Why would it, when subway cars are equally able to be run in forward and reverse? Digging into the answers to these questions gives you the knowledge of how things work. The answer sometimes turns out to be "not that well" or "here's an obvious way to do it better," but you can only get to constructive conclusions after having done the foundational work to investigate how things work.

So, I encourage you to crack open a 10-K (annual report) for a company you're invested in. Learn the constituent parts of that report and others like it. And find out what happens on the floor with that cool name in your own company. You know the one, "Data Operations" or "Security." Or maybe "Marketing and Sales" seems exotic to you. Go find out. Meet the people involved. They'll more than likely be tickled pink at your interest. And the next time you're in an NYC Subway tunnel crossing under a river, ask yourself how and when it was built. The more knowledge you have, the better you will be. As an investor, as a business person, and as just a plain ole regular person.

Chapter 6

Expertise

As MUCH AS I enjoy the thrill of literally every subway ride, most often I am using the subway to get from one location to another in as efficient a manner as possible. Knowing the subway in depth helps me to do so. The intricacies of track layout, connecting station floor plans, and even platform orientation are each an example of means by which the efficiency of a subway ride can be enhanced.

I was reminded of this recently when I had to meet a college friend on the Upper West Side of Manhattan. I grew up on the Upper West Side and I know the subway lines, routes, and stations of the 7th Avenue IRT and 8th/6th Avenue IND lines cold. I knew the time difference of walking from my home on 90th Street to the 93rd Street entrance of the 96th Street and Broadway Station vs. the 86th Street and Broadway entrance of that station. It got to the point where, on that last example, I would instruct my dad, who hated to walk further north to that 96th Street Station when his office was south of our home, on the reason to go against his instinct.

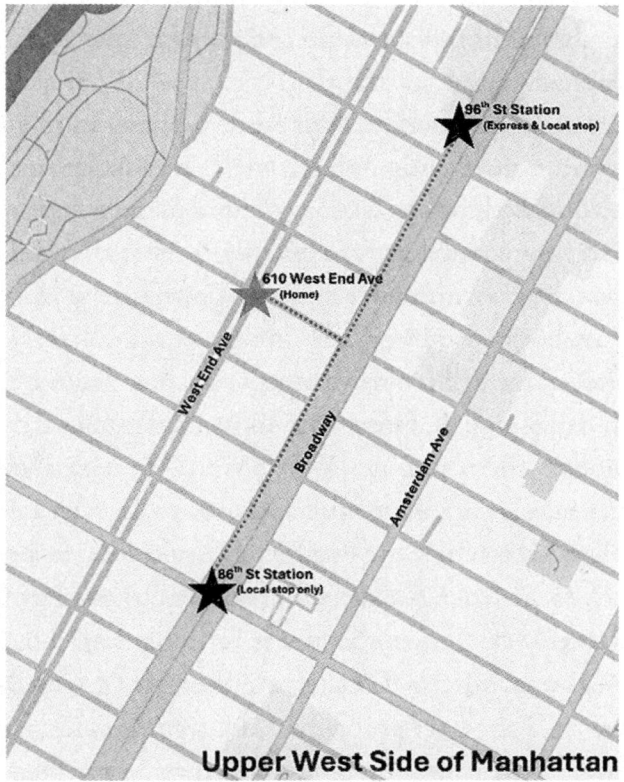

Map Credit: Avalon Lebenthal

Another very important aspect of that 96th Street Station is that both the Express and Local trains stop there. Now, if you're going from the Upper West Side all the way down to South Ferry, you can take the Local train with its twenty stops along the way, all of which are so close together that the train can never get up to full speed. Or, you can take the

Express at 96th Street five stops to Chambers Street and then hop on the Local for the final three stations. Eight stops is a lot less than twenty, and the Express train can accelerate to, and maintain, its full speed along the much longer intervals. Should be a no-brainer, right?

But that connection from the Express to the Local requires graceful timing to bring the trip to its tightest conclusion. Sometimes, that pokey Local is running behind schedule, or it appears infrequently, such that under the most extreme circumstances, it could even be the very same Local that was eschewed at 96th Street completing those last three stops. When that happens, the best route is to not get off at Chambers Street, but to just stay on the Express for another three stops to Wall Street. The two Financial District addresses I have spent the most time in are One New York Plaza, when I worked at Goldman Sachs, and Four State Street, my dad's office when I was a boy. Both are located very close to the South Ferry Station, the terminus for the 1 line, that Local train I mentioned. To take the Express to Wall Street probably adds seven minutes of walking time to the commute as compared to South Ferry. But you can end up sitting at Chambers Street for a full twenty minutes waiting for the Local if you're unlucky. And when that happens, an efficiency-minded subway traveler will rue not having stayed on the Express. What to do? How do we know which path to take?

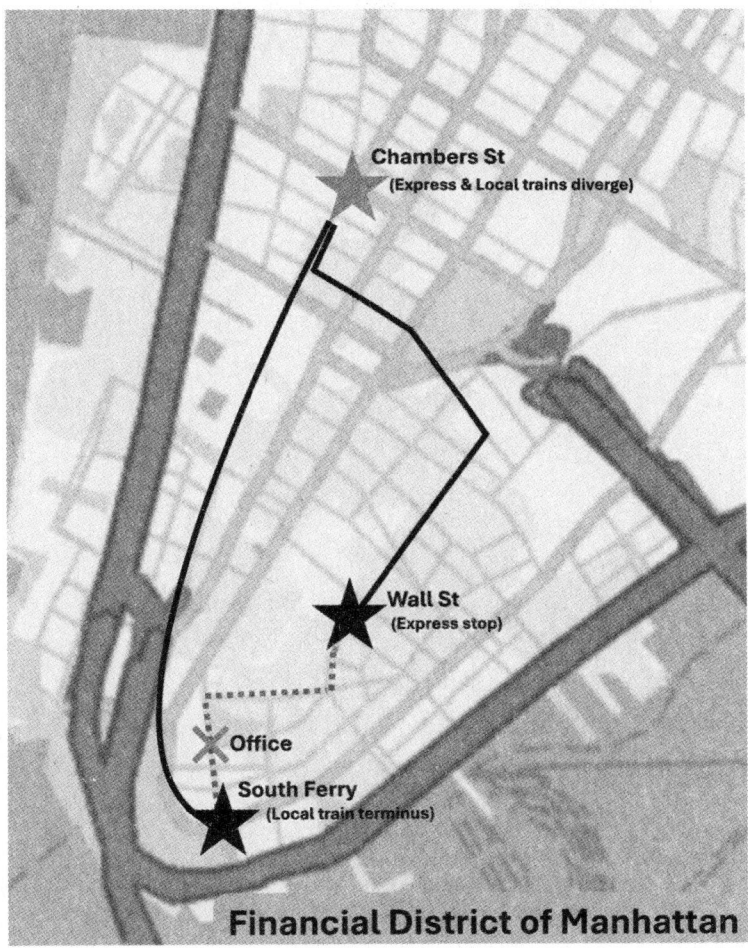

Map Credit: Avalon Lebenthal

I'm happy to say, there's no need for a crystal ball. A little bit of subway knowledge will carry the day. Here's why. The 7th Avenue IRT is tracked between 96th Street and Chambers Street as a one-level, four-track right-of-way.

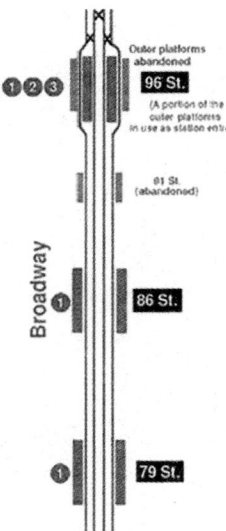

Map Credit: Peter Dougherty, Tracks of the
NYC Subway www.nyctrackbook.com

This means that as the Express hurtles along, you can see
whether you are passing a Local train along the way. If you're
worried that you might have missed one, you can also look at
the signal lights on the Local tracks for clues as to the where-
abouts of that connecting Local train.

Photo Credit: Caseyjonz

Photo Credit: Jim Lebenthal

The NYC Subway uses what's called "block signaling." Those signal lights that you can see when you look down the track indicate whether the "block" of track moving ahead to the next signal is occupied by a train or not. If the light is green, there is no train ahead and any train can freely move forward. A red signal means the immediate block ahead is occupied by a train. Yellow is, as with a traffic light, a caution that, while the block ahead is unoccupied, it wasn't too long ago that a train was in it.

The logic of the signal lights goes thusly: If you see a red light on the Local track, you know there is a Local train just ahead. And since the subways have a reasonable amount of spacing between them, to allow time for passengers to accumulate in the stations before boarding, you can deduce that a train won't be immediately entering that block of track. So, if you pull into Chambers Street, or any station where you want to make a Local connection, and you are not sure if a Local will soon be coming, look at the signal down the Local track. If it shows red, a train just left, and it's likely to be a wait before the next Local train comes. So, you may want to stay on the Express, even if it means a slightly longer walk. That may turn out to be faster than waiting for the Local. A green light tells you that it has been some time since a train was in the station. The green signal is a bit vague though. It doesn't tell you how long ago the train left the station, just that it's been long enough to clear the red signal from the block of track ahead.

Nuances to the above process abound. For instance, don't be fooled by an orange light in the signal box located within the station, halfway down the Local platform. That signal box only contains two lights: red and orange. Green is missing. These signal boxes are a way of telling the Local train motorman that he is not supposed to go full speed through a station where passengers are likely just a few feet away from the platform edge. So, you have to look down the tunnel in the direction the train will go to get a useful indication. At times, this has made people observe me quizzically as I lean over the tracks, looking in what they consider to be the wrong direction. Most people look down the tracks in the direction from which the train will come to see the headlights of an approaching train. My method looks the opposite way to determine how long ago a train left. So far, no one has ever mistaken me for an international tourist and redirected my gaze.

Also, this methodology will only work in a four-track layout where the Express and Local trains run side by side. Unfortunately, that is not always the case. On some lines, such as the Lexington Avenue IRT or the 8th Avenue IND, the Express tracks run on a lower level, below the Local tracks. You can't see either the Local trains or the signal boxes from the Express train.

That knowledge of how the Local and Express trains interact, where the subway station entrances are, how the signal lights work—it all came through repetitive observation, followed by asking *why*. Why is the platform signal light never green? Why is the wait for the Local train sometimes so long? Observing through experience, asking questions, and diligently pursuing answers gives you knowledge. Knowledge that you can apply to your benefit.

Now, why am I feeding you this subway esoterica? Because it illustrates a point that applies to investing, working amongst your peers, and life generally. Be an expert at something. Acquire and hone your expertise, whatever the subject may be. Commit and dedicate yourself to understanding your craft in detail, through experience.

No investor gets every call right, and I am no exception to the rule. I run a portfolio comprised of twenty-five to thirty-five stocks at any time. It would be lovely to think they would all go straight up in price as soon as I buy them. That is never the case. To my chagrin, some go down. And when that happens, I have to explain to clients and to viewers on CNBC exactly why I bought that particular security at that particular price. That requires knowledge. Knowledge of industries and their key performance metrics. Knowledge of what a company's competitive edge may be. Knowledge of revenue growth rates and target profit margins.

I bought my first stock when I was twelve years old. (Okay, my dad did the buying for me.) I had neither knowledge nor experience. But I realized the stock market was a place I could put my brain power to work to generate financial returns and I wanted to learn! I wanted to gain expertise! I learned the best way possible: by doing. Back in those (good ole) days, the newspapers had a dozen pages or so that were all just filled with tiny-font stock quotes. From the prior day's close! This was well before the internet, mind you. There were all sorts of curiosities in those tables that have long since been conscribed to the dustbins of history: corporate bonds listed on the New York Stock Exchange, stock listings from defunct venues, such as the American, Philadelphia, and Pacific Stock Exchanges, share prices quoted in bizarre increments of quarters, eighths, sixteenths (teenies), and so on. It was a tsunami of new terms that I had to learn the meaning of. I will admit that some of my first purchases were a bit quirky: Husky Oil had a cool-sounding name—let's go for it. But I learned what mattered to stocks in the same way I learned about subway block signals: by observing and asking why.

Knowledge was a precious commodity to the twentieth-century investor. The classic 1983 comedy *Trading Places* epitomized this concept. The crux of the movie was commodity investors getting a jump on the market for orange juice futures by early (and illegal) receipt of crop reports. Doing the same in legal fashion was how good investment returns were made.

As an example, when I left the Navy in 1997, I started working for a couple of old-school investors who had founded a firm to invest for clients. These were people who would literally hire someone to buy international newspapers in Europe and fly them over to the United States to get market-breaking news before the US papers picked it up. Heck, on occasion they would even have that courier call in the news from a pay phone at JFK!

My very first professional investment mission was at the direction of Ed Levy and Michael Harkins of the eponymous investment firm Levy, Harkins & Co. I was to call every urologist in the phone book to find out what they thought about Vivus, a pharmaceutical company working on treatments for erectile disfunction (ED). As often happens with new treatments in the pharmaceutical world, ED treatments had become a fad. The same had happened a decade earlier with anti-depressant drugs led by Prozac, and has been happening in the current day and age with GLP-1 treatments for obesity. In 1997, Viagra was less than a year away from US Food and Drug Administration approval. That drug ushered in a raft of treatments for a condition that few had been willing to talk about. But the urologists who treated patients with ED were sure willing to talk about it.

It was amazing how many were willing to talk to a guy basically cold-calling them at work. A few asked if I would compensate them for their insights, but the majority just talked and talked with little prompting from me. I think they relished being in demand when their medical field normally attracted no attention. These doctors pointed out that the Muse treatment from Vivus had an obvious flaw: It was a suppository that no one would be willing to use once comparable medicines in pill form came out.

Back then, access to knowledge was the key determinant to stock market success. Today is different. Thirty years of ever-increasing internet capability has made information ubiquitous. The dawning of the age of artificial intelligence (AI) further enhances not just access to information, but how to integrate it into predictive conclusions. Long gone are the physical Yellow Pages I thumbed through to call those urologists. And the SEC rule Regulation Fair Disclosure (Reg FD) is twenty-five years old. No sell-side analyst has access to company information that the rest of the world doesn't have, at least not legally.

The key to investing today is separating out the signal from the noise. In a sea of information, figuring out what matters is essential. And don't think you know everything.

Nobody does and that's not the point anyway. Separate the wheat from the chaff in terms of what you take into your head. That's what makes great investors and great leaders.

I want to make sure an important point is not lost in what I am saying. Even though we are inundated with information, you still have to gather it into your cranium before deciding what matters. Young investors often ask me to divulge the tricks of our trade. Read voraciously, I tell them. *The Wall Street Journal, Barron's, Bloomberg*, corporate annual reports, government economic releases, and so on. It is only with all the informational ingredients in your head that you can decide which will go into the investment meal that you are preparing. In the current state of polarized politics, I highly recommend reading newspapers from both sides of the political aisle. Read a piece in *The Wall Street Journal*, then read an article on the same topic in *The New York Times*. The different perspectives will help you to figure out where the truth lies. The relevance to investing is to examine both the bull and bear thesis of any investment you make.

Here's a recent example of the importance of detailed information, akin to knowing how track signals work. Investors are right now enjoying a bull market that began in late 2022 and has defied many expectations for its imminent demise. The reasons for the pessimism include high inflation, the US Federal Reserve's aggressive interest rate hikes, the resumption of student loan payments, and many others. Stock market bears have been growling through all of this, but they haven't been fed in the form of a meaningful stock market decline. One important reason for the market's resilience? A very strong labor market, with unemployment at a very low 4 percent and corporate America desperate to hold onto the workers it has, as labor supply decreases with baby boomer retirements.

At the same time, the new presidential administration is determined to reduce the size of the federal workforce and is laying off many government employees to do so. Could this create a rapid increase in unemployment and bring on the stock market decline pessimists are calling for? If that is the case, the first sign will come in the weekly release of initial jobless claims. However, the devil is in the details. Many employees have been offered severance packages or buyouts to encourage their voluntary departure. Jobless claims are administered at the state level, and vary by state. Some will not grant jobless benefits to those who are receiving severance payments. Others will. One has to look at the state-specific rules before drawing a conclusion. Again, you have to collect the information. It is readily available on the internet, in a way that my late-twentieth-century mentors did not have. Once you've collected it, the art is in determining what among it matters, that is, what is the signal and what is the noise. Because of the variety of state rules, and their intersection with severance payments, weekly unemployment benefits may not be that helpful in determining the state of the labor market. Better clues may come from retail sales figures, consumer sentiment surveys, or IRS tax withholdings. Collecting the information is step one. Processing it is the vital second step.

At work and on CNBC, I am known for many things. My good looks may not be among them. Having relevant facts and the ability to put them to use is, I hope, one. But another important aspect of expertise is knowing your limits. We all recognize that one person at work who's got an opinion about everything and is not afraid to voice it at the slightest provocation. He dilutes his message by being so vocal and never seems to recognize that liability.

The biggest liability in being an expert is thinking that it can enable you to tell the future with certainty. So many times, I hear someone say on CNBC that he knows what the outcome of a certain event is: what the Fed will do to interest rates, how a company is going to announce earnings, the level of a future macroeconomic report. In early 2023, when the Federal Reserve was about two-thirds of the way through its unprecedented rate hike campaign and Silicon Valley Bank went under as a result, many people confidently predicted that a US recession would occur as a result. I would listen to macroeconomists speak of their "models" that gave 100 percent-certain predictions of imminent disaster. I debated many of them on air, taking the other side that the combination of supply-chain reshoring to America and government-funded infrastructure spending would keep the economy humming.

In the end, I was right. The economy has stayed out of recession as I write two and a half years later. Of course, I could have been wrong. My intellectual opponents weren't dumb. They were simply too confident in their analysis. No one can predict the future with 100 percent accuracy. When you hear such a certainty, you should always examine the alternate outcome carefully.

Recognition of the inherent fallibility in predicting the future was taught to me by one of the masters of investment wisdom: James Grant. Jim is the editor and publisher of *Grant's Interest Rate Observer* and author of several books on the financial markets. He has an uncanny ability to synthesize historical patterns and current investment environments. I was fortunate enough to spend some time with Jim immediately after leaving the Navy. It was he that introduced me to Ed and Michael of Levy, Harkins. I've never forgotten when Jim put a hundred-year chart of the S&P 500 in front of me and asked, "How far into the future do you feel you can confidently predict what will happen next on this graph?"

I came up with an answer. I can't remember what it was. I think it had the number two in it. Two weeks? Two years? Two quarters?

"Really?" he said, his expressive face morphing into incredulity, eyebrows up, eyes widened, and a wry smile on his face.

His sardonic visual message was clear and needed no further explanation. You can predict with certainty exactly *no* amount of time into the future. Sure, you can express probabilities of occurrences, but you fool yourself, and hopefully no one else, if you profess absolute knowledge of what has yet to unfold.

It was a difficult and yet invaluable lesson for me. I had just left the world of naval nuclear submarines, an exquisite training ground for engineers. In a nuclear reactor, you have such a high probability that a certain isotope of uranium atom will release a certain number of neutrons when split that it seems a certainty. Functionally, it is a certainty. As is the ability of certain alloys of steel used in submarine hulls to withstand crushing pressures which, in turn, are known for given combinations of water depth, heat, and salinity.

I now had to adjust to the world of financial markets in which, on any given day, two plus two doesn't always equal four. On any given day, a company may release fabulous earnings figures, only to see its stock price decline on concerns about the next quarter's guidance, a highly subjective quantity. Alternately, shares of a company losing money, with a highly indebted balance sheet, and neither management nor strategy equipped to turn it around, may soar to unimaginable heights on the back of social media virality. GameStop, anyone?

The best solution to this conundrum for me is to take the approach of a long-term investor. Pick stocks and position your portfolio using engineering-like principles: business models with moats to competition, strong balance sheets, experienced and competent management teams, and shares priced with a margin of error, not priced for perfection. While these principles will not pay off on every day, neither will any investment philosophy. More to the point, if you identify your core principles in investing, diligently research which companies espouse them, and then live with the discipline and patience to hold them to completion, you are likely to be rewarded. For me, this is the solution to putting hard-won expertise to work in a future that will always be uncertain.

Having expertise in a field as uncertain as investing doesn't mean you know everything. At work, I especially love when younger colleagues ask me a question that I can answer with "I don't know." It allows me to challenge their youthful assumption that there are solid answers to every question. Hopefully, it endears me to them, as I give them license to play with possibilities instead of certainties. Of course, I've got to follow that up with some elucidation of what I believe may be the answer.

It's fun when you know your way around the subway system. You know where there's a rise in a particular station's pavement that might trip you up. You know how long it takes to transfer to a different line within a station, whether you can make Track 4 of the Times Square Shuttle or should wait for the next one. It's the same in investing and in work. You know when a stock is trading heavily. Or the markets are. And at work, it's fun when you come into your own on the basis of your knowledge, experience, and judgment. Co-workers respect you. They laugh at your jokes. They like being around you. You don't always have to advertise yourself by opining. Try it. Try not being a know-it-all, but a know-the-right-stuff kind of person.

Chapter 7

Be Careful

RIDING THE SUBWAY CAN be dangerous. Tons of steel hurtling down the tracks, deafening noise, the cars shaking to and fro, the precipitous height from the edge of the platform to the mungy track bed, vermin, heat, steep stairwells, rapidly closing doors. All these can give a palpable sense of fear when you enter the subway system.

But as in business, in investing, and in fact, in the natural world, the biggest danger is your fellow man. As exhilarating as I find riding the subways, the vast majority of my fellow passengers don't care a whit about my passion. They want to get to work, or get home, or pick up their kids. The delivery guy with his bike blocking the front window in the first car is not likely to take too kindly my request to ask him to move so I can stand where I can look out. The guy nudging me with his backpack as we jostle down the tunnels doesn't care too much whether he's inconveniencing me. Expecting empathy from your fellow subway rider is not a winning proposition.

And that is to say nothing of the individuals actively looking to harm others in the subway. They have been there from time immemorial. New Yorkers of a certain age remember Bernie Goetz, the subway vigilante who in 1984, perhaps inspired by Charles Bronson's *Death Wish* movies, took justice into his own hands, shooting four teenagers who were trying to mug him on a subway. In the modern day, the threat of robbery has been augmented by an even more sinister threat: mentally imbalanced passengers who cause random harm. Whereas a rider can tell from experience when he is being sized up by criminals, it is not so easy to determine who is so out of touch with reality that they may visit harm on you. Innocent passengers have been pushed in front of trains, slashed with knives, and even set on fire in recent months. The subways continually remind us of their inherent danger.

I often feel in life that lack of empathy from those around me can be described as people not seeing me as an actual person. Their actions often seem as if they have mistaken me for a cardboard cutout of a person. Someone with whom, from whom, and to whom they feel no obligation to treat as a being identical to themselves. As with most lessons in life, I learned this the hard way. The backpack reference I just made happened to me. I asked the gentleman to move to give me more space, since he didn't realize his backpack was jutting into me. Instead, he aggressively jammed it more into me and invited me to discuss it further with him at the next platform stop. Not the outcome I was looking for.

Similarly, in investing you cannot count on other investors to look out for anything other than their own interests.

Short-sellers may pound your stock into the ground over a disappointing quarterly report before it rebounds on the basis of a well-thought-out long-term thesis. An even better example is when a company has two classes of shares with unequal voting rights. Such a situation can allow a single investor to gain much larger control over the company's destiny than her economic interests in it should allow. I had this happen to me recently with an investment in Paramount, the film and television media company. I believed the company's content library, combined with its strong presence in news and sports, would allow it to transition from legacy delivery via cable and theaters ("linear delivery") to the more modern version of streaming app delivery. Subscribers rapidly came to the service, and a few other things went right, too, such as the blockbuster *Top Gun* sequel, and a CBS-broadcast Super Bowl that went into overtime, generating significant extra advertising income (CBS is owned by Paramount). From July 1, 2023, to March 31, 2024, Paramount generated about $1 billion in free cash flow. Yet, during that time frame, the shares lost about half their value.

How could this be? Well, the company was originally the creation of a talented media mogul named Sumner Redstone. When he died in 2019, his daughter, Shari Redstone, took control of the company through Sumner's ownership of Class A shares, the owners of which, while having the same economic rights as common shareholders, have ten times the voting power. For quite a bit less money than her fellow shareholders, Shari Redstone could do what she wanted with the company. And what she did was a textbook lesson in how to destroy value.

The first thing she did was to lever up her own personal wealth by borrowing money against her shares. The company had a decent dividend with which she could fund interest payments. When the company, under ill advice, cut its dividend in the spring of 2023, the shares naturally declined. And the sharks smelled blood in the water. Recognizing that Shari might face a margin call and be forced to dump shares on the market to meet it, short-sellers beat her to the punch, knocking the price of the shares down hard. But that was only her first mistake.

Next, Shari made it clear to the world at large that Paramount, as a whole company, was up for sale to the highest bidder. Under certain circumstances, that move can work, but you have to be coming from a position of strength. With the dividend cut, she had been forced to sell other assets to stay out of trouble with her lenders. She was running out of time and assets, though, and everyone knew it. Consequently, bids were slow and low in coming. The pressure ratcheted up.

In a final move, Shari and her advisors hatched a harebrained scheme in which an independently run studio named Skydance would buy her control shares for a hefty premium over their value in the stock market. With control in place, Skydance would then order Paramount to buy *it*, Skydance, for about five times more than it would be worth, based on comparable public market valuations. The second transaction would be financed by issuing shares on the open market.

I remember being on CNBC when this was brought to my attention. *What in the world?* I thought. Who in their right mind would issue shares so far below their fair value? And doesn't everyone know that if you announce a share sale ahead of time, the shares are likely to go down as front-runners sell, forcing more shares, more dilution to raise the same amount of cash? All during this so-called deal-making process, leaks to the media occurred at a rate I'd never seen before. These included factual and fictional reports on other potential bidders, legal hurdles, and the emotional volatility of various stakeholders. In short, Shari Redstone had lost complete control of both the narrative and the process.

If that sounds like it's not how deal-making is supposed to go, you're right. But when a desperate controlling shareholder has her back to the wall, anything is fair game. And that's why investors are advised to be as wary of a dual-class share structure as you would be of asking a screaming man on the subway to quiet down. Sure, it can turn out all right—Google and Meta are two successful examples of dual-share class companies—but they are successful *in spite of* that poor governance structure, not because of it. Usually, the situation is far more likely to end in tears. Currently, Skydance owns the control shares it purchased from Shari Redstone. The Skydance purchase by Paramount has been consummated, but it seems probable that remaining shareholders will litigate the deal for years to come. While the ultimate viability of such suits cannot be projected, it may create a big hassle for the company and for Ms. Redstone. At present, Paramount is attempting to go it alone, continuing on as a stand-alone business. Considerable damage has been done by the controlling shareholder, though. As a parting gift, Shari fired the CEO of the past five years who had led the company's transformation. Three executives are serving as "The Office of the CEO," a bizarre leadership structure. Safe to say, most business consultants would recommend a solitary leader. We'll see how easy it is to find a new one, given the governance circumstances.

The point is that danger lurks in investing and the business world. Riding the subway can offer guidance here. The biggest lesson to learn is: Don't take unnecessary risk. The South Ferry Station used to be a place where the 1 train would reverse course via a very sharp loop track. The platform to board and exit the cars was situated along this loop. The short radius of the curve created a large gap between the platform and the car doors, too large for passengers to safely cross. To rectify this, movable gap fillers that looked like interlocking combs would slide out to allow passengers to cross and then slide back in to let the train in and out of the station. One day, my father saw a young boy (not me) who decided to "ride" the gap filler as it receded once the subway doors had closed. He got tripped up and fell into the gap. It was a critical error because when the train started moving, the end of the car would only clear the platform by a few inches. The poor lad would be pulverized. Thinking quickly, Dad reached down and plucked him out from certain doom. I am so proud of him, my original entry to the subway, for that and many other reasons. I sometimes try to picture myself doing his heroic act, hoping I would have the foresight and gumption to succeed.

As I watch the news and social media today, I see stories of subway surfers. One of the worst ideas in the world, this is when kids, usually teenagers with still-developing amygdala, climb on top of moving subway cars. Calling it "surfing" makes sense since they need to lean into the curves to stay on board. But what happens when the subway makes an unexpected track switch and the train lurches sideways? Or when a low-hanging signal post is missed by the surfer? The results are usually fatal.

My strong advice, for investing, working, and riding the subway: Don't go looking for trouble. Believe me, it's hard at work trying to find you. Don't make it any easier to get to you. I doubt anyone reading this is tempted to ride atop a subway car, but you need to brace yourself before getting on the train. Most of your fellow travelers are not likely to be your friends. It happens from time to time that your eye wanders and someone mistakes you looking at him in a challenging way.

Here are some investing activities that I recommend staying away from, just as I recommend you don't ride between subway cars:

- **Leverage:** Yes, if you watch sensational movies like *Wall Street*, in which billions of dollars of wealth are created by borrowing to invest, you may think this is an easy path to riches. The simple truth is that most people don't understand how to manage leverage:

when to cut your losses, when to double down, when to take risk, when to pull in your horns. More people get damaged by thinking they are Gordon Gekko than actually get rich.

- **Options—Part 1:** Publicly traded stock options represent the right, but not the obligation, to buy or sell a particular stock at a set price at any time before a set expiration date. Options have some very beneficial hedging uses, both for investors and for business people. For instance, buying puts on an existing position can protect against downside, and commodity producers can use options to lock in selling prices of their future production. The problem is, the average investor doesn't know the proper techniques to use options. While options can be looked at as insurance for existing positions, most investors fail to continue using them when they prove unnecessary. This is the classic "Why should I keep paying for fire insurance when my house doesn't burn down?" fallacy. Even more perverse is that the cost of rolling protective puts, which means renewing the expiring option/insurance position, usually goes down as more and more time goes by without calamity, only to rise sharply when markets go haywire. Thus, investors usually give up paying for insurance at exactly the wrong time.

- **Options—Part 2:** Besides hedging, options can be used for speculating. Calls/puts have embedded leverage to upside/downside moves in a stock. The payoffs can be tremendous but the probabilities are low. Studies have shown that some 85 percent of all options expire worthless. You are more likely to lose than win in options trading. Combine that with the gambler's fallacy which states that traders on a winning streak mistake luck for skill and continue trading far past a reasonable point, and you can understand my advice to tread very cautiously around options. Recent "improvements" to options, such as "zero time to expiration," have made clear the similarities between options and gambling. Please step back from the edge as the train enters and leaves the station. Don't take unnecessary risks.

- **Options—Part 3:** As I write these admonitions, I bear in mind a number of good friends I have in the industry who actually are quite accomplished in successfully trading options. They have years of experience, from which they have an innate feel for how to balance risk versus reward. They know when a trade has an asymmetric risk probability that is skewed against them. Selling, or "writing," options is one such category. When you sell a call/put, you give someone else the options to buy from/sell to you a specific stock at a specific price. Your reward is fixed in the premium you receive on the sale. The risk however, is very variable. In writing calls, for example, your risk is infinite. The stock could go to unbelievable heights, at which you would have to buy it, only to sell it for the fixed lower price. For this reason, selling calls needs to be hedged with the underlying stock. Writing unhedged or "naked" calls is not for the novice investor. Keep your hands and feet inside the subway car at all times.

- **Short-Selling:** Short-selling is when you borrow a security and sell it, with the intention of buying it later at a lower price to return to the original owner. It is the buy-low-sell-high paradigm, only in reverse. Short-selling plays an important role in the stock market: It enables true price discovery, particularly when bad things are happening. But it has two very big problems associated with it. The first is that, like the unhedged call-writing just described, it exposes the seller to potentially limitless losses for limited upside. It's an asymmetric trade tilted against the short-seller. The other risk is more pernicious: It is one of emotion. I've been a short-seller before. In the early 2000s, when Enron's accounting scandal led to the discovery of many companies engaged in illegal activity, I noticed suspicious accounting entries at Adelphia Communications, a Northeastern cable company. I took a short position and started telling people about the shenanigans I thought were going on. I became engrossed in the stock, waiting for the story to break. Eventually, it did and the short position made money, but that period of time waking up every morning looking for awful news sat ill with me. When you have an active short-sale, you become very negative as a person, very pessimistic. You wake up in the morning hoping for bad things to happen. This way, the stock you've sold short will get knocked down and you can make a profit. It is a very crass, cynical way of making money and it affects your personality. I don't like the way I think when I sell stocks short. For both these reasons, I stay away from it.

- **Speculative Investments:** Meme stocks, special purpose acquisition companies (SPACs), pink-sheet stocks, money-losing start-ups: These are investments that can't be valued by commonly acceptable frameworks and often have "promoters" touting their potential. In the old days, the touters were boiler-room operators, so called because of the tight confines—often in basements—where con men would cold-call en masse, selling dubious investments. Today, they have been replaced by pseudonymous posters on social media or trolling texters. The stock market has more opportunities to get mugged than you might realize. Stick to the lighted areas of the station and be aware of your surroundings. You can make plenty of money in blue chip stocks.

- **Rapid Trading:** I don't know any successful day traders. Do you? Probably not. I'm sure there are some, and I'm equally sure there aren't very many of them. The profession, if you can call it that, of rapidly trading in and out of stocks, came of age in the late 1990s when online trading companies obviated the need to call in your trades to a live broker. Studies have shown that just 1 percent to 3 percent of day traders consistently make money from it. To prove the point, go online and search YouTube for the E*TRADE Mr. Dinky commercial. Don't think that hopping from this stock to that based on what talking heads are saying is the way to make money.

What is true in the subways and investing is true in the workplace as well. Sad to say, there are always going to be some people who have it in for you, no matter who you are or where you work. Zero-sum people who measure their own success in terms of other people's failures, close-minded people who can only see their perspective on life, and outwardly hostile people abound. Not that long ago, I boarded a semi-crowded subway. I could have sat on the bench except one man had his bags on it. When I politely asked if he would move them, he in no uncertain terms told me what I could do to myself. Frankly, it was a rarity for me to ask someone on the subway to behave civilly. If they are showing that they are pre-disposed to selfish behavior—listening to music through speakers, leaning against the stand pole so no one else can use it—then my instruction to them, or anyone else's for that matter, isn't going to change them. In fact, it could set them off. The message? Don't go looking for trouble.

Instead, surround yourself with empathetic people, those with the decency to see matters beyond their field of vision. A couple of years ago, I felt that one of my fellow contributors on CNBC had crossed the line. There's a fair deal of ribbing on my show. Most people look at it as good-natured busting of chops. It's easy to forget that there are viewers out there watching, some of whom are clients, colleagues, and family members. When the teasing goes too far, it can make a person look foolish to these important constituents. I asked this person to be careful and just take it down a notch. I did so fully bracing for a backblast of why it wasn't his fault, that I was being too sensitive, and so on. The sort of response when you would ask someone on the subway to listen to his iPhone through headphones. Still, I felt the lines of decent conduct had to be established, so I went for it, and prepared for a fight.

My colleague's response? "No problem," he said, "I don't want to make you look bad." He promised to tone it down to a still fun, but respectful, level. It took him literally less than ten seconds, but he won me as a fan for life. It's that easy to be that person, but for some it seems so hard.

In each of these chapters, I've endeavored to take a lesson learned in the subways and apply it to both investing and getting along in corporate America. The lesson here, that not everyone is going to care about you, is prevalent in my business experience. Some may argue the contrary, but I believe I have been successful in the Navy, in companies I've worked for, and in media. Let's be clear, though. Any time that I may have been inclined to appeal to the humanity in a professional colleague to get something done, it has often ended in failure. Much like the subway rider leaning his whole body against the pole, preventing anyone else from hanging on to it, the vast majority of people are in this for themselves. Again, they look at other people almost as images on a TV screen as opposed to real-life beings with feelings to which they might relate.

This is not to say that I haven't met incredibly selfless, empathetic people in every institution I've been associated with. And I have made unbelievably wonderful lifelong friends in the process. It's just: That's the minority. Nor does it mean that all is hopeless, that everything is a crass cauldron of Machiavellian what's-in-it-for-me experiences. What it does mean, though, is that you should learn what makes people tick. You can politely ask the guy against the pole to let you have some space. It may work. If it doesn't, move on. And if you're talking to a TV producer about your needs and desires, you darn well better put it in terms of what will make the show better, so it gets higher ratings. If you're talking to your CFO about why you think you should have a higher travel and expense (T&E) budget, you darn well better start by listing the growth rates of your business and how it directly relates to T&E.

We're living in a time where civility is at low tide and yet continues to ebb. A casual drive down the highway tells you as much. Many factors are at play here. Vitriolic political discord. Shooting wars across the globe. A pandemic shutdown that accentuated a YOLO (you only live once) egocentric attitude. Inflation. The list goes on and on. Despite what I see around me, I always try my best to relate with empathy and sensitivity to my fellow travelers on Earth. What I've learned from the subway, investing, and business is that if they don't want to reciprocate, you can't convince them to. It's best to just steer clear. It will be their loss.

And lest that sound incredibly fatalistic and cynical, I am reminded of a kind young woman who noticed that the backpack I was carrying on the subway was open. With a charming smile, she told me and suggested I close it. She reminded me that not everyone on the subway is going to reach in your open bag to rob you. Her genuine concern carried the day, similar to my CNBC colleague's earnest desire to help. It doesn't take much. Often, it's just a smile and a word of care. It can even happen on the subway. And even more important, just because it can be dangerous doesn't mean you should not ride the subway. Obviously, most people need to ride it to get to work. My whole point in this book is that the subway can be thrilling, adventurous, enlightening, and enrichening. Just like investing and being part of a company can, too. I hope to show you that in this book. Read on!

Chapter 8

Explore

THIS BOOK COLLECTS MANY anecdotes from my childhood in New York City. In preparing to write it, I went back and recreated one of my seminal subway experiences: the trip from the Upper West Side to Coney Island that my beloved cousin Annie would take me on. It is a long trip by subway standards. It traverses most of Manhattan, crosses the East River, and covers most of the large borough of Brooklyn. It has underground segments and elevated lines, crosses the Manhattan Bridge, and has broad sections of half-sunken cuts that traverse myriad vibrant neighborhoods. On the trip, festive anticipation of the amusement park builds as the seashore draws visibly near. On the way back, majestic visions of the Manhattan skyline feed a different but still palpable excitement as they steadily grow on the horizon until extinguished by the return to underground as Manhattan closes in.

The ride was as thrilling for me at fifty-five as it had been at age eight. After crossing the river, the subway emerged in an elevated section to cross the Gowanus Canal. Several subway lines are concentrated in this area and, given the visibility of the normally subterranean routes, the tracks snake across, under, and over each other in a way mimicking an intricate roller coaster. Indeed, that is the feeling I get when looking out the front window of the subway: that I am on a thrilling amusement park ride. The exhilaration, for me, permeates the entire system. Switching yards, abandoned stops, intricate and maze-like stations that connect disparate lines—all these things caught not just my attention but my imagination. I knew which platforms had windows into the control rooms through which you could watch the trains approach in '70s technology fashion via slow-moving, analog red dashes on a screen.

The name Darius McCollum probably means nothing to the average New Yorker. To subway aficionados though, he is somewhat of a legend. Slightly autistic, Mr. McCollum also had a fascination with the subways. Though in his case, it went too far. Although not an MTA employee, on multiple occasions, Mr. McCollum "stole" a New York City Subway train, sometimes driving it with passengers. Obviously, there is a certain level of incompetence amongst subway workers to let that happen. And, I hope even more obviously, I would never condone such illegal activity. Having said that, I can easily say I understood Mr. McCollum's activities. He had the same fascination I had, albeit as an autistic man, he was missing some of the behavioral governors that law-abiding subway fans have. To this day, there is a little bit of risk in driving with me on highways near subway storage yards. My eye naturally wanders to the array of trains. But knock on wood, I've not been involved in any crashes because of that!

Now what, you may ask, has all that got to do with investing and with business? The answer is simple. I've just described the playful art of exploring! When you explore, you engage in lateral thinking. Lateral thinking is a manner of solving problems using an indirect and creative approach via reasoning that is not immediately obvious. It is the practice of letting your mind wander, but with a purpose. Let me give you an example.

In 2009, when the proverbial wheels were coming off the global economy thanks to the Great Financial Crisis, I happened to be reading the 10-K (an SEC filling akin to an annual report for a publicly traded company) for Winnebago, the recreational vehicle manufacturer. In it, I read that a good portion of Winnebago's liquid assets were tied up in an investment called preferred auction rate securities (PARS). I had learned about PARS earlier that decade during my time as an investment advisor at Goldman Sachs. PARS were long-dated municipal bonds with interest rates that were reset at intervals as short as one day via an auction process (hence the name) in which investors expressed their desire to purchase or re-up their holdings at certain interest-rate levels. The shortness of the reset intervals, and the ability to fully redeem at those moments, enabled PARS to be considered a cash equivalent by accountants. But the market meltdowns of 2008 and 2009 caused some of these auctions to fail, as not enough investors were willing to roll over their proceeds, given credit-worthiness concerns of the issuers. Once an auction failed, the short-term liquidity feature went away, and with it the ability to consider PARS as cash equivalents. The accountants at Winnebago took note and not only moved the PARS investment to the long-term investments category but, very important, they placed a valuation discount on them. Their imputed price reduction reflected that, at the time, anything other than US Treasuries was regarded with a much higher possibility of default than just a few months earlier. Even my beloved Metropolitan Transportation Authority (MTA) subway bonds were trading at triple-tax-free rates of 6 percent, while the US Federal Reserve slashed interest rates to zero. Investors in Winnebago shares took note of the change and the price of Winnebago shares plummeted due to the dramatic reduction in cash liquidity.

But I thought, based on my explorations at Goldman, that I knew some things about these PARS that the accountants, and the market in Winnebago shares, did not. First, the failed auctions were likely temporary and, if not, the securities could always be refinanced by the issuers with new, different cash-like vehicles. Second, and very important, the prospectuses for these PARS mandated that in the case of a failed auction, penalty rates of up to three times the prior interest rate would be paid by the issuer. This feature, too, would accelerate redeeming the securities and providing liquidity. Finally, I knew that many of these issuers were either essential services providers, like the MTA, or were government authorities with tax-raising abilities to back their debt. In short, these PARS were likely money-good and the discount applied by the accountants, while appropriate, was likely to end up being reversed. The investment in Winnebago shares successfully bore out this thesis and gave me excellent returns.

In the long-term, value-oriented style of investing that I espouse, one is continually looking for a dollar's worth of value selling at a meaningful discount. Exploration is critical to success in this pursuit. I've just highlighted one super powerful way of exploring: reading a company's SEC filings, particularly the 10-K, before investing. It never ceases to amaze me when well-heeled investors plunk down a good sum of money for a company's shares based on what some analyst or someone in the media said. Would you buy a car that way? Of course not! You'd go take it for a test drive, kick the tires, see how it feels. In short, you would explore. And that is a critical part of investing. So dig into those 10-Ks! They are chock-full of tasty nuggets, such as in-depth business descriptions, risk factors involved, and management's analysis of recent business results. Read the footnotes. The footnotes contained the information on Winnebago's PARS.

Similarly, explore your colleagues at work. The easiest way to do this is to accept their invitations. If it is to sit down with them for lunch in the pantry at work or to share thoughts about projects you may be working on, the ability to connect with your coworkers is exploration as well. Recently I was invited to run in a 5K charity race by a new friend at work, Lisa. I didn't know her all that well, but her poise and intelligence were readily apparent. She explained the organization behind the event: a financial literacy advocacy group, helping young and underprivileged students to learn about investing. Sounded like a great cause to me!

Maybe she thought I would be a hard sell, but I jumped at the offer. I've always been a runner but, as I've gotten older, my stamina and pace have dropped off. I figured a good, low-key race would be inspiration. I was right, and in more ways than one. Lisa invited more of the office to join the race, using it as an opportunity to bring together people who didn't often interact together. Some were young, some were older. Some looked like they could really run, others looked like they were out for a nice stroll. The race was along the Hudson River on a beautiful summer evening.

To say I had a blast is an understatement. The group of us from Cerity Partners bonded in the anticipation before the starting call, cheered each other on, and gasped (okay, well maybe just I gasped) for breath upon completion. The out-and-back route allowed us to see who was leading on the backstretch and shout encouragement. Afterwards, there were well-earned back pats and we all headed to a local pub for celebration. That evening, over the shared exertion and bit of liquid encouragement, I found out more about my colleagues than I ever could have by bumping into them in the office pantry. I have a better feel for their goals, motivations, desires, and fears. I see them in the multiple hues of their lives beyond office cubicles, and I draw inspiration on a daily basis from them. I would not have gotten this benefit had I not accepted Lisa's invitation.

I want to tell you another story about exploring relationships through the simple act of accepting an invitation. Unfortunately, this is a lesson about what can happen when the invitation is not accepted, at least not in a fully committed way.

I wrote in Chapter 3 that I used to take the subway after school as a preteen to sing in a local church choir. My invitation to join that choir came from a classmate, David. David and I had attended Trinity School in New York City for several years up until then. Trinity is a well-regarded K–12 private school, offering a well-rounded education with excellent preparatory skills for college education at top universities. The classes were small—about sixty students in seventh grade, my level at the time. Most of them looked like me. David did not. David was one of the few kids of color in our class.

When he invited me to join in the choir, I agreed. We would take the subway together. David commuted to school every day by subway. He took different routes than I was used to and so he was able to show me different aspects of the subway than I had known about. Some of these were the sensory aspects of the subway. We would get a hot pretzel at a stand near the Times Square Shuttle platform, that station filled with food vendors, the sounds of music, and seedy newsstands. He introduced me to garlic and onion potato chips. He also gave me one of the biggest scares/exhilarations of my subway experiences when he and I stood in the vestibule between two subway cars as the train was moving. The roar and wind of barreling down the tunnel made my heart beat faster than it ever had.

After nine months, I quit the choir. I can't remember a momentous reason for the decision. It had just run its course in my life. But I then made a mistake. I did not develop the friendship with David further. This wasn't a conscious choice. He lived far away from where I did and we were in different classrooms most of the time. Our paths simply didn't cross often anymore.

About a year later, during one of the rare times our paths did cross, David and I got into a fight at school. Who knows what started it. The teachers separated us and we never talked about it. I thought he was the aggressor, but there are two sides to every story. It took me many, many years to understand what his side of the story was. I believe that, in short, he was hurt that our friendship dissipated. And while in 1981 I thought he had acted like a jerk, in the fullness of time I realized he was living a more difficult life than I could comprehend. He didn't fully fit in at Trinity. For him, our friendship had been an oasis in the sea of loneliness that he felt at Trinity. I was too young and naïve to understand any of that. I write about it now to hopefully—hopefully—prevent it from happening again, in my life or in someone else's. I hope David reads this chapter and recognizes it as the paean to him that it is.

Seek knowledge through your explorations. There is a difference between knowing something and knowing how to apply it. That is the difference between facts and wisdom. But you have to start with the facts, especially the ones you don't know. So let your senses wander when you ride the subway. Take in the unique underground feature of the 137th Street storage yard on the Broadway IRT. Imagine the surfers, in their wetsuits with boards in hand, on the A train causeway across Jamaica Bay heading to the Rockaway shore and the Atlantic swell. Walk across the bridge between the Times Square Shuttle and the 1 line, understand that the shuttle is a segment of the first NYC Subway line built, and then go to the Grand Central end to look for its track connection to the 6 line. When you have knowledge, you can then connect your facts in patterns that display intelligence. Intelligence that will serve you in investing, in getting along in business, and in being a human being among others.

Sometimes your explorations may lead you astray. I wrote earlier of the time with my mother at the South Ferry terminus of the 7th Avenue IRT when we were looking to board a train back home to the Upper West Side. I was convinced I knew more than I actually did and somehow got us on the abandoned inner platform of what had decades earlier been the shuttle to Bowling Green. Thinking that this service was still active, I convinced my mom to wait for a half hour until she correctly deduced we were not where we needed to be. That South Ferry Station has since been replaced and the Bowling Green platform boarded up, but I still can't help but look with fascination behind the façade at what once was. The point is, exploration leads to experience and knowledge, two attributes that, when combined, lead to insight.

So go grab that 10-K of your favorite stock and find out something the rest of the world doesn't know. It may end up making you money. And accept the invitations that come your way, especially—and I mean especially—the ones that may seem the goofiest. They often come from the most charismatic people you will meet. And if you need inspiration for all of that, hop on a subway, not to go anywhere in particular, but just to look out the window. In a word, explore!

Chapter 9

Serendipity

IN THE INTRODUCTION TO this book, I wrote about my very first subway experience, taking the subway with my dad downtown to his office. The impact of watching the train come down the tunnel from very far away made an amazing and exhilarating impression on me. We were at the 96th Street Station of the 7th Avenue IRT, on our way to the southern end of Manhattan. The train was coming from the north. At that quite young age, I had never really experienced the north end of Manhattan. We lived on 90th Street, and all major events in my family's life—dining out, visiting museums, seeing relatives—took place south of where we lived. Sure, if we were driving out to the country we might go north on the Henry Hudson Parkway, but that was removed and insulated from the actual city that existed past 90th Street. To me, that first train was like a wild barbarian rushing from the northern hinterlands into my civilized world.

As I got older, I gradually would explore points in Upper Manhattan and the Bronx. School sporting events were often held at Van Cortlandt Park, an oasis of natural beauty in the city. Its cross-country tracks are literally world-renowned, and it has athletic fields galore. Randall's Island was another sporting venue. In fact, it was the home field for my school, Trinity, when we played interscholastic lacrosse games. This was in the mid-1980s, way before its renovation. These were hardscrabble fields. As hosts, we would have to arrive early to pick broken glass off the fields and line them with chalk. To call them fields at all was a bit of a stretch. Probably half was bare dirt. We considered it our home-field advantage to play other schools used to playing on perfectly manicured greenery.

These were the first forays I made into the wild steppes of northern Manhattan. Immediately after college, many classmates and friends took apartments in the area, drawn by attractive rents, and I would visit them when home from the Navy on leave. As many of them and I were avid runners, we would run along the Hudson River to the George Washinton Bridge and back. Sometimes, we would go even further north and then take the subway back south. It was on one of these trips that something magical happened for me.

It had been a particularly good run, long and fast. I was tired, so I did not take my usual position standing at the front of the first car to look down the tracks. Instead, I sat on one of the seats, which were set up along the length of the car, so that the view was out the side of the train. I looked forward to one particular oddity of this subway route: a fourteen-block stretch where the tracks come out into the open to cross the Manhattan Valley while keeping a level grade. Anticipating this, I was attentively watching the passing tunnel through the side windows. But just before we reached that landmark, a new curiosity appeared.

Photo Credit: Aspersions

Seated along the side of the train, my view of the nondescript tunnel walls suddenly deepened. Steel supports showed the route expanding by many tracks, most with stationary trains parked on them. I looked behind me and saw a similar effect on the other side. This was my first glimpse of an underground railyard at 137th Street. I realize not everyone will share the same sense of excitement at this discovery as I had, but I can tell you I was thrilled. Plenty of people take this subway line every day to get to work and, for them, whatever excitement they may have had about the yard at first has long passed. However, I find subway yards fascinating. They are all over New York City and give you glimpses into the trains that you can't see from the dark, narrow confines of the underground stations. There's the 207th Street Yard along the shores of the Harlem River, easily seen when driving north on the Major Deegan Expressway out of the city. On your way to John F. Kennedy Airport from Manhattan, the Jamaica Yard is chockablock to the Van Wyck Expressway. In each, you can see the variety of different types of subway cars. Non-revenue generating trains, like maintenance and cash-collection units, are easily distinguished by their Day-Glo yellow-and-black paint schemes. Massive repair facilities with spaghetti-like connecting tracks loom large. To an engineering geek like me, it is hard not to stare. There are twenty-four subway yards in the NYC Subway system. But to this point, I had never imagined there were underground railyards.

Some of you will understand the fascination I felt at finding that underground facility, some will not. "Urban exploration" is the term for those of us who delve into those hidden, sometimes abandoned, manmade structures, such as rail depots, catacombs, or ghost fleets. This type of exploration is typified by the serendipitous nature of discovery. You turn a corner, traverse an innocuous stretch of subway line, and something unexpected and glorious appears before you. It is that serendipity that I wish to chat about now.

The *Oxford Dictionary* defines "serendipity" as "the occurrence and development of events by chance in a happy or beneficial way." In that definition, the term "by chance" deserves more scrutiny. It is innocuous enough, to be sure. Quite often, the "by chance" nature of events that lead to good outcomes is, in itself, not so good. Quite often, we find ourselves using the trope "as one door closes, another opens" to comfort someone, or ourselves, against whom fate has struck an unhappy blow.

Only, it's not a trope. As I look back on my career as an investor, financial advisor, and business leader, I see clearly now that at each turning point, as disastrous as some of them seemed, the best possible outcome was achieved. Of course, personal agency is involved. One's efforts largely determine the outcome. But faith! Faith that your world will turn out okay or even blessed, when all seems turned against you— that is how serendipity turns chance into success! It is all tied together.

In the beginning of this book, I told you of my investing start as a young lad. Picking up *The New York Times* in the pre-dawn darkness to flip to the stock tables in the back. Wondering what made those companies' shares go up and down. Plunging into investing with dogged determination to figure out how it works. And yet, at first, my professional world after finishing college had nothing to do with investing. It was in the Navy as a submarine officer.

It was in the Navy that I met an array of simply incredible men. These are people who don't stand out in a crowd, but they had enormous impact on me. In fact, in many ways they molded me. When I see them today, they still influence me. I'm talking about captains, fellow junior officers, enlisted personnel, chief petty officers. I would like to think I've been a benefit to them as well.

One individual stands out to me in this discussion about serendipity, though. Bill Frake was the chief engineer on the USS *Oklahoma City*, the submarine to which I was assigned as a division officer from 1992 to 1995. A lieutenant commander at the time, Bill—"ENG" as he was known on the boat—was widely regarded as one of the finest engineers in the Navy I strongly agree with that assessment. Bill had an excellent career, rising to command of the *USS Montpelier* and leading that ship through a highly successful deployment during the Second Gulf War. He was my first boss when I hit the waterfront as a twenty-three-year-old green ensign. He showed me the ropes: what core principles are when operating a naval propulsion plant, how to manage reactors and radioactivity, how to lead men.

I benefited enormously from being under Commander Frake's tutelage. It was pure chance that had me assigned to the same boat with him. And that chance turned into my benefit when he rotated ashore in a coveted billet as a full-time student at The Wharton School of Business to pursue a master's in business administration (MBA). When I came out of the Navy, I decided that pursuing an MBA would both provide a smooth transition back to civilian life and give me key skills to turn my passion for investing into a career. Bill took it upon himself to promote my application within the admissions department at Wharton and was thus instrumental in my being accepted to that prestigious institution.

One of the best things about Wharton was that leading corporations would come to the school to actively recruit from the student body. It was thus very easy for me to interview at Goldman Sachs in 1998. Goldman is a storied firm. Its prestige got dinged a bit during the Great Financial Crisis, when *Rolling Stone* called it a "great vampire squid wrapped around the face of humanity, relentlessly jamming its blood funnel into anything that smells like money." But when I told my father, ten years earlier, that I was interviewing for a job there, he called the firm "the Knights Templar" and said if I could get a job there, it would be amazing for me. I was fortunate to land a summer internship in the equities division, which was basically a ten-week interview process. Ten weeks in which to either screw up or show what you were made of. In two and a half months of close observation, the firm would be able to tell each intern's real abilities and real character.

I made my share of mistakes that summer, but had my successes, too. I was thrilled to be offered a full-time job in what would eventually be the Goldman Sachs Wealth Management business. This was a home run. I would be able to hone my investment skills under the aegis of this fabulous firm. I had amazing mentors. I built from scratch a meaningful client base, and I did it the old-fashioned way: through gritty, determined, thoughtful cold-calling. Not an easy business, cold-calling, but one that makes sense when you view it purely as a numbers game. You make one hundred calls.

Ninety of them don't talk to you. Ten engage you at least in a conversation and, in some cases, a meeting. Out of those ten, one or two become clients. It is hard to bear the rejection rate, but if you have the gumption, it will work out. The character you build in persevering is invaluable.

Wealth Management was brand-new when I joined. In fact, I joined the preceding business model, Private Client Services (PCS), which was more of an institutional trading business designed for the ultra-high-net-worth clients created by Goldman's investment banking business. In the late 1990s, this was a go-go-go business. The S&P 500 averaged 26 percent annual returns in the second half of that decade. The first internet boom combined with a tech/telecom capital expenditure frenzy in advance of the Y2K fears. Realizing that we're talking about three decades ago, I'll describe those two phenomena a bit more. The first internet boom was a period of time when personal computers became ubiquitous, processing power and storage capacity saw dramatic cost declines, and the advent of the internet opened up tremendous new usages for digital technology to connect people, information, and commerce. Amazon, Yahoo, AOL, and eBay were just a handful of companies created out of thin air in response. Existing companies like Microsoft, Intel, and Cisco Systems pivoted their businesses to take maximum advantage. It was an intoxicating time of accelerating profits, technological innovation, and gonzo capital markets, in which splashy weekly initial public offerings created wild overnight riches. For great satire of the moment, it's worth searching for E*TRADE year 2000 ads. They are hilarious send-ups of the moment.

The moment was added to by the looming end of the millennium. "Y2K" refers to the fact that during the second half of the twentieth century, the dawn of the digital age, computer software had been ubiquitously coded so that dates used only two numbers for the year. Thus, July 20, 1969, was coded "072069." What would happen when we reached January 1, 2000? Would all these digital systems reboot to January 1, 1900? The potential havoc created a spending boom on new software, hardware, security, and connectivity amongst the global IT ecosystem. The revenue and profit increases at technology and telecommunications companies were extreme. A little gravy was added in a nationwide replacement of copper telephone wires with more efficient fiber optics.

For PCS, it was a marvelous time. The trading floor on the top floor of One New York Plaza would create overnight tech millionaires from moonshot IPOs, and the PCS brokers one floor down would scoop up all their new investing business. Only, it was a dangerous time too, in that it had to come to an end, and when it did, its decline was likely to match its ascent. It always does.

To the credit of Goldman Sachs's management, they foresaw this and smartly changed strategies to prepare. The transition from PCS to Private Wealth Management meant detaching from the trading atmosphere and moving to a chief investment officer model, in which client-facing professionals like me no longer advised on individual securities but instead picked other investment managers, mostly external to the firm, who would pick stocks, bonds, and so on. The value an individual in my role provided was in devising financial plans, establishing asset allocations, managing trust and estate advice, and so on. That's actually a marvelous business and core to my current firm. However, it relegated me to a bystander role in the security analysis process, the part of the business I loved—the stock-picking I had done since age twelve.

For some, that would have been a terrible blow. To land the perfect assignment at the crème de la crème firm, only for the firm's strategy to shift right under your feet. In the end, it was a clear case of serendipity. I left Goldman Sachs to pursue the path I dreamed of: being a professional equity investor.

My first move was to go to Levy, Harkins & Co., the investment firm I had interned at during business school. It was a fabulous opportunity to learn at the knees of grizzled Wall Street veterans. Yet while I learned a lot, the culture wasn't right for me. It was a small firm, seven people. While the stock analysis acumen was off the charts, I found myself alone in my office far too much. I craved more human interaction. My stay there wasn't long, though, because again fate would intervene and change my course for the better.

When that course change happened, it didn't feel like it was for the better. I had a falling out with my partners over investment strategy. Clients I had gathered during my Goldman days were leaving. The parting was difficult and I felt regret. Should I have left Goldman to begin with? It was a high-risk move. Stories of successful transitions from

Goldman are plenty, but what do you hear from those who left and never again reached those heights? History, as they say, is written by the winners. Where would I go next? Would my remaining clients come with me?

Then along came fate. My sister, Alexandra, and my father, aka the municipal bond king, were restarting the family business and asked me to join them. Lebenthal & Co. had a storied history in the twentieth century as the go-to shop for individual municipal bond investors. But the new millennium and the rise of investing super-shops made the Lebenthal focus on one investment type obsolete. After a series of mergers, Lebenthal & Co. was digested in the maw of investment giant Merrill Lynch around 2005. Not to be deterred, my sister and father restarted the firm. Determined not to be a one-trick pony, the firm augmented its municipal bond bona fides by adding equity management, which I would lead, and wealth management.

I spent a decade working at the new Lebenthal with my sister and my father who, after an impressive tenure on Earth, passed in 2014. I made a whole host of new friends who are both investment gurus and life coaches. One of the most magnificent gifts that came from this period was my introduction to CNBC. When I talk about serendipity, the random chance occurrence that leads to something great, this is what I am talking about.

My father had been an incredible marketer. He was a well-known figure in finance through print, radio, and television. My sister had some of the same skills, and augmented them with her formidable networking acumen. Through her, I was introduced to CNBC one day and invited to appear on the 5 p.m. Eastern *Fast Money* show, a roundtable talk show about the financial markets, economy, and individual stocks. I was asked to pitch a stock and I chose Caterpillar. I don't remember why or what my overall position on it was. Strangely, I just remember focusing on projecting some small financial detail, such as research and development spending, three quarters from then. Whatever I said, the producers seemed to like it. They invited me back the next day to do a different stock and then again after that. The next few months, I would appear on this show and the noontime *Halftime Report*. I couldn't tell the rhyme or reason for the invitations and I fully expected that each appearance would be my last. As the old saw goes, if the phone didn't ring, I would know it was them (CNBC). There was no instruction manual—this was not operating a naval nuclear plant. I learned by doing, and by making mistakes. Then, I started receiving schedules for my appearances for the month ahead. What had been ad hoc became regular. A few months later, when I was seen in a one-off appearance on a competing business news channel, CNBC made it official. I became an exclusive CNBC contributor and a starting member of the *Halftime Report* lineup.

CNBC has been supremely positive for me. Sometimes people will say to me, "Gee, they really seem to give you a hard time on the show." I will admit the edginess was initially sometimes hard to take. Sometimes it still is! But the truth is, the producers, the managers behind the scenes, and my co-contributors are all wonderful. Despite the sharpness of our debates, we each have profound respect for one another. I have learned an incredible amount from each of them, about both investing and how to be a person. At the top of the list is the show's anchor, Scott Wapner. Scott gives people the business when they avoid admitting mistakes and especially when they try to BS their way through something they don't know. He holds all of our feet to the fire. I've seen him do that with CEOs, politicians, legendary investors, and us on the committee. If you don't answer his questions, you will not get away. Integrity, insight, and intelligence are hallmarks of Scott and the show. That is precisely what makes the *Halftime Report* the best show on the network. I'm not just saying that! It is often the highest-rated show on the network. Scott brings out the best in us. And when you consider the cast I have to work with—Josh, Jenny, Steph, Steve, Joe, and others—that best is a hell of a lot.

The final step in this saga is how I came to be at Cerity Partners. Cerity Partners is a rapidly growing registered investment advisor (RIA) firm. I joined the firm in 2017 when it was less than a decade old and just coming out of proof-of-concept mode. Eighty people were managing $9 billion in client assets in a handful of offices across the country. As I write in the summer of 2025, we are 1,300 people and with our affiliates have over $130 billion in assets under management, but doing so through an array of different services including investing, financial planning, tax and accounting, trust and estate advisory services, and many others. We provide a holistic approach to our clients' wealth, taking care of them in ways and with a quality that I think no other firm can match.

More than anything, though, I am blessed, truly blessed, to work with an incredible collection of colleagues. Before joining Cerity Partners, I would never have imagined that there could be such a unified esprit de corps across so many people doing such a myriad of functions. From the newest hire to our senior leadership, there is a human decency that can only be described as family. In the dog-eat-dog world that is Wall Street, that is truly unique.

Wall Street routinely goes through business model "fads." When I came out of business school near the end of the tech/telecom boom I've mentioned, it was all the rage to get a spot on a big Wall Street firm's research team. Sell-side analysts were rock stars. Until Henry Blodget at Merrill Lynch killed the business model by trading the objectivity of his stock ratings in exchange for investment banking business. The luster of research analysts faded. But have no fear! Wall Street followed that up with hedge fund managers, then private equity managers, as rock stars.

The RIA sector may seem faddish today. It is one of the top areas in finance that graduating students want to pursue most. We are never short on summer interns and when a full-time job opening gets posted, it is inundated quickly with applicants. Cerity Partners is among the largest independent RIAs in the country. But none of what we do seems faddish. Having a fiduciary interest in putting our clients first, accessing the best investments—the same as the biggest pension funds get—at the most attractive pricing possible, continually innovating to bring the latest technology in monitoring risk and presenting results, these are just some of the core principles by which we work. The combined ethos of an RIA gives meaning and purpose to someone like me. Ultimately, we are taking excellent care of our clients and their families. There is nobility in our goals and passion in our efforts. Try as I may, words do not fully convey that the mission and the people at Cerity Partners make it the best place I have ever worked (navy submarines excluded from the comparison). I am way too old to be "drinking Kool-Aid"—Cerity Partners is truly special.

And how did I get there? You guessed it. An unexpected and unpleasant turn of events. After ten years working with the family, the new Lebenthal corporation became unwieldy. We were trying to be too many things to too many people with not enough resources. Our capital partners wanted to merge with bigger firms with more resources, but a deal couldn't be struck. We could plod along, performing at an average level in our various business lines, and we tried to do so. For me, the joy of taking exquisite care of my clients and growing a business was getting subsumed in leases, debt negotiations, and hiring decisions. My clients felt neglected. I was not in a position where I could be my best professional self.

It was then that I was introduced to Kurt Miscinski, the CEO of Cerity Partners. Kurt had a vision. It was clear, it was powerful, and it was attractive. He was building the pre-eminent wealth management and professional services firm. A firm to last in employee-ownership form for generations to come. In a ninety-minute discussion, Kurt laid out the mission, the milestones, and the incentives. A few days later,

I came back to meet key partners and stakeholders. I was quickly sold. Kurt is, in my opinion, a unicorn. He has an incredible mission on which he is clearly focused. He has built up a firm with a very large number of like-minded people. With him, we are tireless in our efforts. In short, I am the happiest I have ever been in my professional investing career.

When I interviewed to join Cerity Partners, my role on CNBC was a selling point to the firm. It gave national name recognition to the otherwise unheard-of start-up. My appearances gave comfort to firms that joined us that we had real marketing presence and clout. My presence on CNBC would not have come had I not joined my family's firm. I would not have joined my family's firm had my time at Levy, Harkins & Co. not ended. And I never would have joined Levy, Harkins had I not taken the plunge, taken the risk of leaving the vaunted Goldman Sachs, which in turn had stemmed from the Navy, Bill Frake, and Wharton. Do you see how every event leads to another, even though each shows nothing more about the future than the next step? There is a trust in that process. It's a belief that any blow you face will be returned with a blessing. For every door that shuts, another one opens. I have seen this throughout my life. I earnestly believe in it. Trust and gratitude are the foundations of success.

I know that in this chapter, I haven't really detailed any particular stock or investing methodology. This chapter is a bit lengthy, as I've gone through how all the pieces of my career have come together. There's certainly stuff I've left out. Ask me sometime about how an expensive pair of skis factored into my decision to join the Navy. The common thread in all of this? How each transition felt tumultuous, scary, risky, and yet, at the same time, fully exhilarating with the sense of opportunity, the ability to expand my horizons through them. Many of the moments felt downright perilous. And yet they led to greatness. And one couldn't have happened without the other. Goldman Sachs taught me marvelous lessons about investing and building a business advising clients. But I could never have done the CNBC appearances with Goldman. It just wouldn't have fit Goldman's corporate ethos. I had to take the risk of leaving Goldman to reach my final destination, not even knowing at the time what that was. And I am sure that there are more transitions ahead. They may feel life-altering and negative, as it did when I left the embrace of my family's firm. But they have inevitably led to a better life for me.

So, the next time you're on the subway, and you catch a glimpse of the unusual with your peripheral vision, don't ignore it. Turn to it, lean into it, and see what wonders await you. If it seems scary and uncertain, don't fall for that. More often than not, you'll be happily surprised with what fate has in store for you. There's magic in what I'm telling you. I want you to believe in that magic. I've seen it work countless times for me. I'll bet it will for you, too.

Chapter 10
Bad Things Happen

IN LATE OCTOBER 2012, Superstorm Sandy smashed the Northeastern United States. It was an incredible meteorological event that was severe enough to cause the New York City Subway system to shut down entirely for two days, an exceedingly rare event. The track of the storm and its high wind speed combined to create an enormous storm surge that was perfectly aligned with the entrance to New York Harbor. Normally well protected by the Verrazzano-Narrows, the harbor suffered a perfect strike. The tip of Manhattan saw the water level rise by a record of almost ten feet. This was significantly higher than the surrounding city seawall.

Seawater poured into lower Manhattan and Midtown. The subways, being below ground, naturally acted as drains for the floodwaters. Tunnels to Brooklyn and Queens were completely filled. By the time everything was pumped dry, the subway's infrastructure was damaged catastrophically. Track beds were undermined and unstable. Track signals and electrical wiring were beneath the salty, corrosive seawater for days. In the end, major sections of the subway would be closed for months at a time. This was a major blow to a system that prides itself on twenty-four-hour, seven-day-a-week service.

Bad things happen. We live in an imperfect world, a world of barely controlled, and sometimes entirely uncontrolled, chaos. The proverbial butterfly flaps its wings and causes a cyclone halfway around the world. It's true in the subway, it's true in the stock market, and it's true in business. If you're trying to control your life in any of these three regards so that you will never face hardship, forget it. It can't be done. There is no level of control, analysis, or prescience that will prevent bad things from happening. It doesn't even have to be as monumental as Superstorm Sandy. Several times a week I head to the Grand Central Station stop on the Lexington Avenue IRT to take me to Wall Street. There, I disembark to head across Broadway to enter the New York Stock Exchange where we air *Halftime Report* on CNBC. The show starts at noon Eastern. I can leave my office in Midtown at 11 a.m. and be there in time to get my makeup done, grab an espresso, and get mic'd up with ten minutes to spare. That's how efficient the subway ride is. Unless it isn't.

Sometimes, I get down to the platform at Grand Central and see a big crowd waiting for the train. That's a clue that something may be amiss, that it has been a while since a train has arrived to clear out the waiting passengers. Often the next clue is an announcement: *Due to equipment problems on the number such-and-such line…, Because of earlier police activity at the such-and-such station...* These are some of the many reasons that trains may be delayed or service even halted. The train status signs can give further information. Anything longer than a five-minute wait in the middle of a business day tells me we're not running smoothly.

Or, sometimes the trains stop in the tunnel and sit. And sits and sits and sits. The clock ticking, your next meeting fast approaching, and eventually occurring without you.

To think you will have a blemish-free life is naïve. I'm fairly certain that life would be insufferably boring if everything went according to plan every time. We don't relish the mishaps, but they make the smoother times more poignant and powerful. The key is to maintain an even keel in both cases: when things go right and when they are off track (pun intended).

When things go right in the stock market, when all your portfolio names are up, and you're outperforming your benchmark by hundreds of basis points, it's easy to get carried away with yourself. You can start to think you are the universe's gift to investing, you can do no wrong. Invariably that's when you take on too much risk, too much concentration in a particular stock or industry sector. I've written about balance in Chapter 13. The balance needs to be struck in your emotions, as well as your actions.

This includes when things are going against you in the stock market. Believe me, there have been times when I have wondered if I am in the wrong profession, if my whole career has been a mistake. Especially for someone who pays close attention to the price paid for a stock and to its valuation, the period since the Great Financial Crisis ended has been difficult. It has been one in which value investors like me have languished. It has been impossible to hide, also, given the public crucible in which my picks are dissected.

And yet, the longer I have gone in this business, the longer simple truths have gotten me through both the exuberance and the despair. These include investing for the long run, buying high-quality companies, and focusing on valuations. Every investor faces times where he feels he's lousy, but by sticking to those credos I have found far more times of success than failure.

Simple truths can get you through more dramatic downturns, as well. In the past few years, we've seen a bear market in 2022 as the Federal Reserve raised interest rates to combat high inflation; 2025 has brought a perilous re-ordering of the global economic order that, as I write, may upend the supremacy of the US economy, the US dollar, and the US Treasury market. Conversations with clients, colleagues, and everyday people on the street show their fear that the world is irretrievably changing for the worse.

Here, again, one must recognize that bad things are unavoidable in the temporal world. As I help clients to navigate the worst of times—the bear markets, the recessions, the governmental catastrophes, the wars—I reflect on how many times calamities have occurred in the arc of my own investment career. The 1987 crash, the Y2K bust, 9/11, the Great Financial Crisis, COVID-19. Each of those had its own unique, intrinsic characteristics. Some were manmade, others the natural result of the economy's boom-bust duality.

The common attribute among all of them? We got through them. By "we" I mean each of us individually, the stock market, and the world collectively.

I doubt that I have seen my last big market rout. I don't waste time trying to control for those nasty moments. The only perfect way to avoid a loss in the market is to never invest, never take a chance. The chance you would be missing by sitting out is that glorious long-term return. If that seems too laissez-faire, consider the downside of simply staying invested through time. History shows that even if you invested right before each of those terrible market events I mentioned above, as long as you stuck with it, the market recovered over time and gave ample returns. Take a look:

$10,000 invested in large cap stocks right before:	Experienced an immediate drawdown of:	But would still be worth this much today:	For a cumulative total return of:	Or an annualized return of:
The Tech Bubble Burst	-49%	$60,204.08	502.0%	7.4%
September 11	-12%	$77,993.54	679.9%	9.1%
The Great Financial Crisis	-57%	$51,809.12	418.1%	9.9%
The COVID-19 Pandemic	-34%	$20,394.13	103.9%	15.0%
The Last Bear Market (2022)	-25%	$12,344.76	23.4%	6.7%

Investment Returns Through April 7, 2025.
Credit: Jim Lebenthal

On occasion, bad things are going to happen to investors. They're unavoidable. You have to accept this reality and keep your wits about you. Don't think you're terrible at it. Just pick what your credos are and stick to them. And remember in the good times, too, to not get carried away by euphoria. I am reminded of this every trading day when I look at the pre-market futures. Often, there is a stock that is responding to great news and sometimes there's one getting pummeled by bad news. Other times, it's the market overall responding to a better-than-expected or worse-than-expected macroeconomic release.

The same thing is going to happen when you are a company leader. I think there is a set of people who believe all you need to do is reach a certain height on the org chart and then you've got it made. Then you don't need to worry about a thing anymore. Not so. At any level, you are going to face hard times, as well as times where it seems you can do no wrong.

I've seen swaggering CEOs like Bernie Ebbers hold conference calls in blue jeans and cowboy boots, only to end up disgraced in prison. In private companies, I've seen the shirttails-to-shirttails-in-three-generations story. In my own experience as a leader, whether in finance, on TV, or in the military, I've always tried for that balance of being confident enough to stand up for myself, while not being so arrogant as to bluff my way out of a bad call. It's about living the Buddhist principal of the Middle Way. As stated in the *Dhammacakkappavattana Sutta* of about 2,500 years ago: "There is an addiction to indulgence of sense-pleasures, which is low, coarse, the way of ordinary people, unworthy, and unprofitable; and there is an addiction to self-mortification, which is painful, unworthy, and unprofitable."

It's so hard to remember that neither good times nor bad times are permanent. When you're stuck on a subway car with broken air conditioning and a funky smell, it's easy to say you're never going to take the subway again. And when you get to the station just as a subway arrives and it effortlessly, efficiently gets you where you want to go in no time at all, you feel like this is the only mode of transportation you'll ever need. You have to remember that neither elation nor despair ever last. Even more important, you have to remember that there is far more of the former than the latter. So, remember that when you see your favorite stock getting crushed after-hours because of a slight miss on one quarter's earnings. It's another lesson I've learned from the subway.

Chapter 11

Change

MANY OF MY FAVORITE places in the New York City Subway system are no longer accessible. The South Ferry terminus of the 1 line, about which I have spoken much in this book, used to have a very sharp turnaround loop by which southbound trains could reverse course to head back uptown. The outer edge of the loop served as the platform. It was a small station, and only half of the typical ten-car trains would platform at the station. I would get off at this station as a kid when I went to visit my father who worked downtown. Later, after the Navy. it was my stop for the four years I worked at Goldman Sachs. I can still hear the conductor's voice as the train travelled south of Chambers Street for the two stops before South Ferry. He would urge passengers to move past his spot in the middle of the train to the first five cars if they wanted to get off. Once in a while, a tourist would misunderstand and question me with panic how they missed the stop. I remember the quirky gap-filler platforms, needed to safely disembark from the cars along the sharp curve. You would come up from the cramped station underneath a ramp leading to the Staten Island Ferry. Next to the entrance was a pizza parlor crammed into a shoebox of a space.

Photo Credit: Kurt Raschke

That loop turnaround station was replaced twenty years ago. The 2001 terrorist attacks on the World Trade Center led to a number of infrastructure improvements in the area. New tracks were built to a deeper and more modern station that did not have a loop turnaround. Trains now come in and then the motorman goes to the rear car and uses that as the lead car to reverse direction. The new station can fit the full trains. No more panicked tourists pulling the emergency brake as the South Ferry platform whizzed by them. Much easier connection can now be made to the Staten Island Ferry, and there is a free in-station transfer to the BMT Whitehall Station with trains into Brooklyn, Manhattan, and Queens. The charm of the loop turnaround station is gone, but it has been replaced by something more efficient.

A similar example is the recent modification to the Times Square end of the Times Square-to-Grand Central Shuttle. This shuttle is a remnant of the first subway line which went from City Hall up the Lower East Side to Grand Central Terminal before sharply curving west along 42nd Street to Times Square. From there, it curled back to the north, heading up Broadway and the West Side to Harlem. The separation of that original line into today's constituent segments was an improvement that was made before my time. The renovation that I am discussing, though, happened in 2020.

The change was necessitated by the quirky manner in which the station had to be designed when the shuttle was first established. So that the shuttle trains do not get forever marooned on an isolated track between their two stops, connections still exist to the 7th Avenue IRT at Times Square and to the Lexington Avenue IRT at Grand Central. This way the trains can get to the yards for maintenance. As you can see in the subway-map excerpt, it is the northernmost shuttle track that connects with the 1-2-3 lines and the southernmost shuttle track that connects to the 4-5-6 lines. This means that the full four-track right-of-way had to be kept active for the shuttle. This is more than a little overkill for a route that runs back and forth between two stops. Two tracks would suffice, one going each way at a time.

At Times Square, an additional problem is that when the shuttle comes in on that northernmost track (Track 4), passengers have to hightail it over a movable platform to get to the boarding platform. The movable platform is pretty cool, though, as it is actually in the operating tunnel of the 1 line. When the northbound IRT Local goes by, you can almost reach out and touch it.

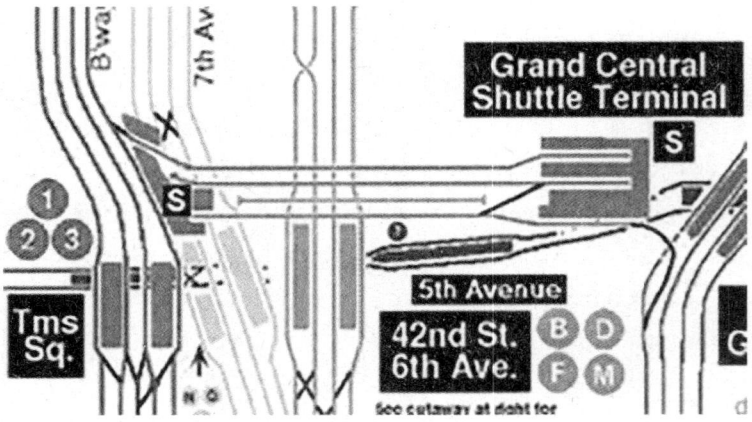

Map Credit: Peter Dougherty, Tracks of the
NYC Subway www.nyctrackbook.com

Passengers would not head over to Track 4 unless they saw the next train to Grand Central was leaving from it. But during the time it took to hoof it over the moveable platform, the waiting shuttle on that track might depart without them. Disappointed passengers would then have to hoof it back over the moveable platform to board a shuttle on one of the other tracks, hoping it, too, would not depart prematurely without them. There was a little bit of stress in all this. I know. I was there.

So, in 2020 the Metropolitan Transportation Authority renovated the station. Track 4 was taken out of service. Service was reduced to two trains on two tracks, a much more economical set-up. The two tracks are now serviced by one island platform and there is no need for a passenger to "guess" where the next train departs from. It is, all in all, a much better design.

Except that that moveable platform has now been walled off. You can't see it and you can't get to it. It may seem like a minor loss, but not to me. I loved walking across that platform, being in the actual tunnel. It gave me an absolute thrill, feeling like I was in a forbidden zone, the operating tunnel. As with most of these anecdotes, I realize the sadness I feel over its being bricked up is not shared by all. And there is a solution to it, which I will get to at the end of this chapter. But first and foremost, we have to discuss what change is, what it means.

Human nature is to always look for what isn't working efficiently and try to improve it. We live in a highly imperfect world. Opportunities to improve it abound. Consider trading in US stocks before the deregulation of commissions in 1975. Before then, the New York Stock Exchange charged a fixed commission for every trade, regardless of size. Every brokerage firm abided by the schedule. When this system was abolished in 1975, it opened the door for competitive commissions. With this change, new firms like Charles Schwab, Quick & Reilly, and others soon made a business for themselves marketing cut-rate commissions to investors. Old-school brokerages feared their businesses would be destroyed by the new entrants. In important ways, they were. Settling trades took a full seven days before reregulation and even then, it wasn't enough. The stock exchange would sometimes have to shut down on a trading day to clear a backlog of unsettled trades. The system was sclerotic but there was no incentive to do things differently. The change helped to create a more vibrant trading environment. The upstart discount brokerages knew that to be profitable at a lower rate, they had to make it up on volume. They innovated to make the system more efficient. Overall stock trading volume picked up. In 1975, the dollar volume of all stocks traded in the United States was $137 billion. In 1985, it was eleven times higher at $1.47 trillion. With the increase, deeper and more liquid markets gave better pricing to investors.

The effects of deregulation found their ultimate form in online trading systems that came of age in the 1990s. Smaller investors, like me when I began, had been forced to invest for the long term, in part to recoup the sizeable fixed commission charged on smaller trades. Now, with commissions close to zero dollars, investors could easily buy and sell on the same day. The concept of day traders now meant that rapid-fire trading could allow profit from miniscule price changes on the same day.

Today, the concept of paying for trading is hilariously antiquated. But, as with all change, there are unintended consequences. Studies have shown that the average investor benefits more from a buy-and-hold strategy than from rapid trading. There are very few day traders from that phenomenon's first heyday in the late 1990s who were able to make a career out of it. During the recent pandemic, many young investors stuck at home found dopamine-triggered solace in trading through mobile apps. Their tales of trading success found ample audiences in social media. In the end, gambling favors the house, in this case the large market-making firms that pay for the order flow generated from all this trading. When day traders run out of money, they don't post about it on X.

Commission deregulation is one of many seminal changes I've witnessed since 1980, when I first bought a stock. Online account access, real-time pricing, portfolio performance measurement, and exchange-traded funds are some others. Many of these innovations were made possible by that deregulation and the competitive power it unleashed. The phenomenal increase in computing power in my lifetime has made these improvements possible. The investor's world is better off for them. I still have a few clients who prefer paper statements. When they inevitably ask how many years' worth they should keep, I hear them wondering why they do it. As for me, I miss the old bankers boxes in which I kept paper statements—*not!*

The rapid advance of digital technology has also made the workplace for more efficient. In the twentieth century, one had to call up a company and request annual reports and proxy statements by mail. Their arrival felt like a birthday present. I would pore through them, gleaning relevant information and marking them up with yellow highlighters and written commentary. I cannot imagine a company today entertaining my request to have physical printings of their SEC filings mailed to me. Well, I can imagine the laughter on the other end of the phone. Today, one downloads a PDF and uses online editing tools to do the same thing I used to do in hard copy. I can't help but think of the evolution of floppy disks to CD-ROMs to USB drives to store all this. There used to be a company called EMC in the late '90s that made gobs of money for offering digital storage. How quaint! There's a business model that evaporated. Data storage costs are effectively zero now.

I can think of no better improvement in the workplace than video teleconferencing, a.k.a. Zoom. The ability to have a virtual meeting with colleagues, friends, and clients has revolutionized the way we work. It was a corporate savior during the COVID-19 shutdowns. Five years after the pandemic, it remains a critical tool for collaboration and efficiency. Firmwide meetings for a firm the size of Cerity Partners would have been held by audio-only phone calls ten years ago. Now you can see the faces of your colleagues, narrate presentations for all to see in real time, and enhance the discussions with online chat and Q&A. Talented workers need not be in the same geographical location to be your teammates. You can easily work and conduct meetings from the road.

And, as with every new revolution, there are unintended consequences. School kids today no longer have the supreme joy of days off known as snow days. No, I'm not talking about global warming. It used to be that when there was significant snow accumulation, classes would be cancelled because it would be unsafe to travel to school. Not anymore. Zoom makes it so that kids have virtual classrooms at home no matter how hard it snows. Sigh.

The dangerous side effect that I see from Zoom-enhanced remote work is foregoing in-person, live contact. People in my firm know that if they pass me in the hall or see me in the pantry, they can ask me something impromptu. State of the markets, good stocks, will the New York Jets ever have a winning season again? Younger colleagues, in particular, benefit from being in the presence of their peers and more experienced team members. They bond with the former over shared tasks, trials, and successes. They get critical mentoring from the latter, the type that is simply stultified in an online format.

Return-to-office has become a hot-button topic, now five full years after remote work became prevalent. I hear the attributes listed for remote work: It enables child care, it widens the pool of talent on which to draw, it removes time spent commuting. These are valid points. To me, they are outweighed by the benefits of being in the office. Unquestionably, Zoom and remote work are valid business tools. Used too much, though, they become a hindrance. Just like too much stock trading in a zero-commission world leads to sub-optimal investment performance.

Yet, even as change brings both improvements and unintended consequences, it also brings sparkling new opportunities.

In other chapters of this book, I've described the various methods I've learned to determine when and where to switch from an Express train to a Local train. These methods always had a degree of error to them. For instance, examining track signals in the track ahead will tell you if a train has just left a station. And there is a correlation such that if a train did just leave the station, then the next one probably will take some time before it arrives. But it's an imperfect system.

It's also a system that has been made obsolete by the new monitors on each platform telling you exactly when the next train on each line will arrive. I now use the monitors every time I travel from my office to Wall Street for *Halftime Report*. If the monitor shows that an Express train won't arrive for another twenty minutes, and there's a Local already in the station, then I take that Local train. Even though it doesn't go all the way to Wall Street, it's a ten-minute walk from the terminus of the Local to the stock exchange. Secretly, though, I still look at the block signals, to keep that skill set sharp, kind of like how a sailor will occasionally navigate by the stars, lest GPS atrophy that ability.

Radical change in stock trading seems to happen every year. We're a universe removed from trading shares under the buttonwood tree (the New York Stock Exchange was created by an agreement made in 1792 under the shade of a buttonwood tree on Wall Street). The list of new opportunities is seemingly endless. Being able to instantly chart moving averages, technical patterns, or order imbalances are things that I could not have even dreamed of when I started in this business. Industry-specific exchange-traded funds, exchange-traded funds themselves, the list goes on. The toolbox for the modern investor could not have been imagined in the 1980s when I started investing.

It is really in the office where I think change has created fabulous new ways to succeed. As mentioned, Zoom teleconferencing kept business going during the pandemic.

But when air travel started to pick up again, I was one of the first to get back on the road. The competitive advantage of going to personally visit clients and prospects was tremendous. Most of the firms I compete with got very comfortable doing everything remotely, probably too comfortable. People really appreciated the extra effort of my coming to see them in person. They, too, craved the human interaction after the shutdown months.

Here's a very easy way to take advantage of all the changes that the digital world has wrought: Send a hand-written letter. It will make a tremendous impression. Think about the last person who sent you a personal note instead of an email. How did that make you feel about them? The modern world gives you many ways to stand out. Sometimes, they are by just going old-school.

And maybe that's a good note on which to close this chapter. I will confess that I have often found change hard. Nostalgia gets me, and I tend to hang onto the old ways of doing things. My solution is to blend the old ways with the new. You can, too. You have to embrace both sides.

In the past few months as I've written this book, I've toured some of the old corners of the subway system that I remember from childhood. Many are now hidden, like the moveable platform at the Times Square subway platform. But with a little moxie, you can get to them. The Lexington Avenue IRT that I take a few times a week contains plenty of Easter eggs: The abandoned 18th Street Station and the gap fillers at Union Square Station are throwbacks to the earliest decades of the subway system. But the grandest surprise of all is the abandoned City Hall Station. This was the first subway station built. It was closed in 1945 because it was too short for the longer trains needed to service an ever-increasing number of daily riders. It is a beautifully ornate station, befitting a European metro station. If you take the 6 Local to its southern terminus at Brooklyn Bridge, and if you ask the conductor nicely, you can stay on the train as it loops through the abandoned City Hall Station. I do it from time to time. It gives me my fix of nostalgia, with which I can embrace the newest improvements to the subway. I'll remember that as I retire my MetroCard soon for the new pay-by-phone feature, just as I once had to give up my subway tokens. Times change and I must change with them. There's nothing wrong with hanging on to the memories, even as we all move forward.

Photo Credit: Rhododendrites

Chapter 12

Dream

THE IDEA OF THIS book rattled around in my head for a couple of years before I put pen to paper. Anecdotes and memories would come to mind. Some were happy, others a reminder of disruptive experiences. A lot of them, though, dissipated before I finally got serious and started to write. To help the creative juices to flow, I recreated one of my favorite subway trips: the ride from the Upper West Side of Manhattan to Coney Island. I've mentioned this journey a few times already, but I want to go a little deeper here.

New York City is unlike any other city in the world, and my city in the 1970s presented an incredible array of senses and experiences. It was dirty and gritty, dangerous and exciting. Above all else, it was authentic. Visitors today have no idea what the Times Square area was like then: a cauldron of despair and opportunity that permeated all its environs, including the subway station with its embedded Latin record shop and news kiosks filled with magazines from all over the world. The block of 42nd Street between 7th Avenue and 8th Avenue was regarded as the most dangerous block in the city. Movie theaters showed karate films, first-run movies, and X-rated titles. Game arcades offered fake IDs to under-aged teenagers, no questions asked. The streets were filthy and menacing. Movies since then have tried to portray the fantastic characters populating this area. None can come close to the real thing. It was awesome.

Many of the city's legendary sporting events are easily accessible by subway. In the summer, spontaneous trips to the old Yankee Stadium for a ball game were easily made by the East Side's 4 line. As you walked downstairs from the elevated line, the scene on the street was a carnival of fans getting lubricated at iconic Stan's Sports Bar under the tracks. In the fall, the Flushing 7 line could take you to Shea Stadium, where the NY Jets played football on a field often still laid out as a baseball field for the incumbent NY Mets. The West Side's 1, 2, and 3 would get you to Madison Square Garden for Knicks basketball and Rangers hockey. Spontaneity was the flavor of the era. If you were hanging out with your friends on a weekend day with nothing to do, you could hop a subway to a home game. Tickets at the box office were always available and cheap, too. If you've ever sat in the bleachers for a Yankees game, you know what I'm talking about.

And for sports you played instead of just watching, those lines would get you up to the ball fields, running routes, and golf courses of Van Cortlandt Park in the Riverdale section of the Bronx. I am proud to say that as a fourteen-year-old I would grab my golf bag and ride the 4 train up to the

Mosholu Golf Course. Sometimes I took lessons. Believe me, that experience was a far cry from being coddled by pros at The Breakers in Palm Beach. If I swung wrong, I heard about it in more colorful language than I can write here!

Growing up in this kaleidoscope of the senses was fabulous. The subway gave easy access to all of this, in addition to its remarkable effects on productivity and quality of life for the city's workforce who could live in more tranquil environs than where their workplaces were situated. One of my frequent companions growing up was my cousin Annie. She and her family lived on Central Park West, a ten-minute walk from my home. Sixteen years my senior, I think Annie got a kick out of showing me all New York had to offer. The Bronx Zoo, Ringling Bros. and Barnum & Bailey circus, March of Dimes walkathons—she could always be counted on to drum up a good time. But no time was better than when we went to Coney Island together.

In America, it seems you're never more than an hour's drive from an amusement park. And most of them are over the top with wildly engineered and gaudy rides. Coney Island in the '70s was more like what a county fair looks like today. It was small in scope by today's standards. The rides were laughably small in comparison to anything a Six Flags Great Adventure would offer. And they had that same feeling of being recently and fragilely bolted together that travelling carnivals have now. I loved everything about it. The three wooden roller coasters (Cyclone, Tornado, and Thunderbolt) were each crammed into a single city block, the cars rattled and jostled as they sped along tracks that had to twist and reverse over themselves to give a meaningful run. The log flume, bumper cars, and carousels were among my favorites. The Wonder Wheel, a Ferris wheel with cars that moved along tracks, gave a cool twist on a classic. The arcades included pinball machines and Skee-Ball games. The food, the skills game barkers, and the wide spectrum of New Yorkers were set against the backdrop of the boardwalk with the Atlantic Ocean beyond. I couldn't get enough of it.

The subway ride to and from Coney Island was a big part of the adventure. So, when it came time to get the ink flowing for this tome, I decided to take that trip once again, this time as a mid-fifty-year-old instead of a little lad. I boarded the F train at 86th Street and positioned myself at the end of the platform to get a place at the front of the train. The view was not as easy as in my youth. Today's subway cars have a full-width cabin for the driver. This clutters the view by forcing you to look through two windows in sequence. It's much blurrier that way, but still possible. The keyhole solution was unworkable. My fellow riders must have thought I was a nut. I secretly hoped they understood my passion and agreed with me for standing and staring out the front car without a pause for the hour-long ride.

During the trip, the memories from my youth flooded in. While underground, watching the narrow confines of the tunnel framed by steel girders fly by, I felt anticipation around every curve. The trip was like an amusement ride itself. In the dark tunnels, it felt like Space Mountain at Disney World, the famous roller coaster in the dark. When we broke into the light, an intricate web of other lines intersected with and separated from ours. The twists and curves felt just like a roller coaster. As my destination grew closer, I felt the growing anticipation and eagerness that I remembered from fifty years ago.

This combination of using the past (boyhood trips by subway) in the present (current trip to Coney Island) to enhance the future (writing this book) is called dreaming. Let's chat a little bit about dreaming in investing. It's a tricky subject. There's a fine line between dreaming and hoping. You've heard the expression "Hope is not an investment strategy." That's true, but it's a little too cynical, at least for me. Dreaming, to me, means not holding back. It means really trying to swing for the fences.

Here's a little more on the distinction. I mentioned earlier that I grew up in a family of municipal bond managers. Visiting my dad at Lebenthal & Co., our municipal broker-dealer, was tremendous fun for me as a kid. Those trips are relevant for many reasons. They catalyzed my affection for the subway, both because that's how I would get there and because the subways were financed by municipal bonds. At the office, I would hear traders and salespeople haggling over the right interest rate to sell a bond. During the late 1970s battle on inflation, some of these interest rates were double digits, a meaningful tax-free rate of return for hard-earned savings.

But those rates of returns were fixed. They would not vary if you held those bonds to maturity. Sure, you could trade them, but few if any retail investors were successful at doing so. Growing up in my family, you owned some of these bonds from an early age. I collected the coupons, at first with great excitement. The thrill soon waned, though. I knew every six months what the interest payment would be. Don't get me wrong, those cash payments were nice to receive. There was just no variability, no change up or down to look forward to. I quickly intuited that the stock market was where I wanted to invest.

There's an academic theorem about the stock market known as the efficient market hypothesis. As the name implies, this paradigm suggests that everything that is knowable about a stock is already known and already priced into the stock. By extension, there is therefore no value in actively picking stocks to try to beat the market. Needless to say, I completely disagree with the theory. I believe that with innovative and diligent research you can find out significant information about companies that is not priced in. I don't know any active equity manager who disagrees with that. It is what we mean when we say that a company will beat or miss its earnings estimates. We believe in an inefficient market.

So, when an investor like me starts a new position in a company, there are projections that we have constructed for the future. Predicting the future is a difficult task, rife with potential failure. But I build my expectations for the company based on a thorough review of financial reports, interviews with management, and analyses of competitors, customers, and suppliers. This is a far cry from simply reading what a sell-side analyst thinks. By bringing in the professionalism, expertise, and experience of which I have written about extensively already, these aspirations for a company become more than hope. They become dreams, dreams that are worth reaching for and have a likelihood of coming true.

My investment in Transocean is an example. Transocean is an offshore drilling company. It leases deepwater and harsh-environment drilling rigs to global oil and gas exploration companies. These drillships and semi-submersible rigs are incredibly complex pieces of equipment. They can remain still despite wind and waves, in waters more than two miles deep while drilling thirty thousand feet to forty thousand feet below the surface. The rigs are complex and expensive to operate. Energy companies engage Transocean for drilling projects budgeted for many years of operations. The rigs cost hundreds of thousands of dollars a day to lease.

During periods of rising fossil fuel prices, exploration companies are willing to pay top dollar to secure access to these rigs. There is a finite supply of them (about 150 worldwide) and building new ones takes years and billions of dollars. When West Texas Intermediate (WTI) crude oil priced above a hundred dollars per barrel between 2008 and 2014, Transocean made gobs of money. It averaged $10 billion in annual sales and its stock soared. Trading at thirty dollars per share in 2003, by 2008 Transocean shares changed hands for $150.

But by 2021, when I did my initial deep dive into Transocean, the shares had collapsed to two dollars. What had happened? Well, there's a saying in commodity industries: The cure for high prices is high prices. The rise in crude oil prices begat new supply. From the early 2000s, shale production in the US took off, aided by new technologies, such as lateral drilling and hydraulic fracturing. Fears that the world was past a point of "peak oil" production gave way to a glut. Saudi Arabia and the OPEC (Organization of the Petroleum Exporting Countries) cartel were used to being able to control supply, and thus pricing, for decades. Unwilling to cede leadership to the United States, in November 2014 they responded by flooding the world oil markets with supply. OPEC's goal was to crash prices below the level at which US shale producers could profitably operate, putting them out of business.

OPEC succeeded in tanking oil prices. By 2016, in less than eighteen months, WTI oil prices collapsed from $150 per barrel in 2008 to below forty dollars. US oil producers were reeling. Years of aggressive spending to expand drilling resulted in financial loss and bankruptcy. Production companies pulled back on capital expenditures to drill new wells. In the offshore business, Transocean saw day rates on it rigs plummet. Where it had been able to charge more than $700,000 per day for the most modern rigs in 2015, two years later those platforms commanded less than $500,000 per day. When COVID-19 shut down the global economy a few years later, oil demand vanished. In April 2020, oil was momentarily quoted in negative amounts. Transocean's fleet fell further in value, commanding $315,000 per day on average.

The company's management recognized that it was not profitable to operate many of these rigs in that environment. Annual revenues came down to $2.6 billion in 2021, almost one-quarter the level of ten years earlier. Profits turned to losses and cash flows went negative. To stay out of bankruptcy, management mothballed much of the fleet. This is when things started to turn interesting for me and I decided to take a closer look.

I had been peripherally aware of Transocean throughout the storyline. No one in equity markets could miss its moonshot of a run when times were good. The act of mothballing its drillships and semi-submersibles was novel. Normally, in a highly cyclical and capital-intensive business, assets like these that had lost their economic viability would have been decommissioned and sold for scrap metal. It never ceases to amaze me how when times get tough shipping companies will beach enormous ships at scrapping yards and airlines will sell state-of-the-art planes for parts. They then have to spend ungodly sums of money to buy new assets when the economy perks up again. Apparently, Transocean management felt the same way that I do, because instead of scrapping these incredible machines, they sent them down to the Caribbean to sit in standby for when times might get good again. No one in the industry had done this before.

Photo Credits: Stephane M. Grueso, Niels Johannes

As of late 2025, the global economy is currently growing, but in a spotty fashion. The US economy is leading the way at 3 percent real gross domestic product growth and 4.1 percent unemployment. Unfortunately, it's not getting much help from anywhere else. China is growing, but sluggishly. The hope is that its government will add stimulus to invigorate growth. Europe is a mess, with individual country economies laboring under higher interest rates and higher unemployment. Uncertainty abounds from a world awash in global conflict and a new US presidential administration. Tariff announcements and a global trade war further exacerbate the situation. In this mixed environment, WTI is selling for sixty-five dollars per barrel, high enough to get exploration companies interested in drilling offshore again. Day rates have started to climb. At the last quarterly fleet status update, Transocean reported that average day rates had climbed to $442,000 per day, with some rigs charging well over $500,000 per day.

Is it enough to get those idle rigs back into service? The market price for Transocean shares is currently less than 50 percent of book value. Book value is the value of all a company's assets minus all its liabilities, as officially measured by its accountants. If a company were to stop doing business, wind up its affairs, sell all assets and pay all debts, book value is what theoretically would be left. Those accountants are carrying the value of the idled rigs at their historical cost less accumulated depreciation. The stock market is saying they're worth a lot less. It's saying they are not likely to come back into service and that, when inevitably sold for scrap, they will net a lot less than what the accountants currently say they are worth.

It is certainly true that these mothballed rigs may or may not be brought back into service. The company actually has scrapped some of the ones it originally mothballed, and maybe they all will be discarded. The bigger point is, I don't believe the market is efficiently pricing in all available information in Transocean's current share price. I dare to dream that those idle rigs will be put back into service, and soon. If I were just licking my finger and placing it in the wind to draw that conclusion, then that would be just hope. As stated, hope is not an investment strategy. No, my dream is based on analysis, on taking the time to find out as many facts as I can and drawing conclusions from the same.

Here are some relevant facts. There is no appetite to build new rigs, given the three-year lead time and $1 billion price tag per unit. The supply of rigs is, therefore, finite. While any increase in oil price may bring the threat of OPEC supply increases, they are unlikely to be of comparable size to 2014. In the aftermath of that move, Saudi Arabia ran a budget deficit equal to 15 percent of its economy in 2015, a truly monstrous shortfall that will be remembered and avoided in the future. The current demand vs. supply balance in offshore drilling, combined with a price that is attractive for deepwater oil exploration, could lead to those idle rigs being brought online. If they do come back into production, their impact on Transocean's finances could be meaningful. Reactivating just five rigs at a currently bargain rate of $400,000 per day would yield $730 million in new annual revenue, a 20 percent immediate increase. At current margins, cash flow would increase by $450 million, or 34 percent. As for the so-called efficient market, I struggle to find a sell-side analyst who believes this is priced into Transocean's current share price.

I use Transocean as an example of dreaming, thinking big, investing. Isn't that the salient metaphor for American business? Consider the seven largest companies in the stock market. These companies—Apple, Alphabet, Amazon, Meta, Microsoft, Nvidia, and Tesla—have a combined market cap of $18 trillion. For perspective, the global economy is $110 trillion. So, these companies represent 16 percent of global productive worth.

These companies, a.k.a. the Magnificent Seven, have been in existence for an average of thirty-three years. Their average age as public companies is twenty-seven years. Think about that for a second. What were you doing in your life between twenty-seven and thirty-three years of age? It is the young-adult phase in terms of human life. These companies were born from dreamers: Mark Zuckerberg, Elon Musk, Jeff Bezos, Bill Gates. They dared to dream and dream big. They are lionized today for what they've built. They and their companies represent the pinnacle of commercial enterprise.

What's more, they serve as inspiration for entrepreneurs around the globe. Entrepreneurial spirit seems written into the DNA of America. My family is one of entrepreneurs. My grandparents started a municipal bond business from scratch in 1926. My grandmother was a female pioneer in an industry dominated by men. My father took over in the late 1960s and dared to dream. He ran prolific advertising to create the Lebenthal & Co. brand. For decades the firm was iconic in municipal finance and in New York City culture. And then, at the beginning of the twenty-first century, new entrants came in and took center stage. Charles Schwab, Fidelity, E*TRADE, and Ameritrade were all younger than Lebenthal. Perhaps it was their youth that unleashed new ways of combining investments and trading. Their one-stop shop for all investments made a specialist firm like Lebenthal archaic, no matter how well regarded. In 2001, the family firm was sold to Mutual of New York (MONY).

In some ways, that end to Lebenthal & Co. felt like a failure. Sure, it was a monetizing event for the family, but after that control of the firm's destiny was lost. MONY was sold to the French insurance company Axa, which in turn hived off the Lebenthal business to Merrill Lynch in 2005.

Dreaming is not dependent on, nor a guarantee of, success. I know no successful business person who hasn't been bruised badly at least once on the road to glory. The key is never letting the failures stop you from moving forward, from thinking big, from dreaming. You cannot stop just because one of your dreams doesn't come true.

There are certainly some forms of dreaming that are more likely to lead to success than others. In investing, I often hear people speak of TAM (total addressable market) or measure a company in terms of its price-to-sales. To me, this is folly. It is ridiculous to compare an individual company to its TAM, as if no competitors exist. And any company can garner sales. All you have to do is undercut on price. Gaining sales profitably is the goal, and that's a totally different subject: earnings. Here are the words of wisdom from Scott McNealy, CEO of Sun Microsystems, a darling of the late 1990s tech boom. In March 2002, after shares had collapsed from a 2000 peak of sixty dollars to below ten dollars, he wrote:

> At 10 times revenues, to give you a 10-year payback, I have to pay you 100% of revenues for 10 straight years in dividends. That assumes I can get that by my shareholders. That assumes I have zero cost of goods sold, which is very hard for a computer company. That assumes zero expenses, which is really hard with 39,000 employees. That assumes I pay no taxes, which is very hard. And that assumes you pay no taxes on your dividends, which is kind of illegal. And that assumes with zero R&D for the next 10 years, I can maintain the current revenue run rate. Now, having done that, would any of you like to buy my stock at $64? Do you realize how ridiculous those basic assumptions are? You don't need any transparency. You don't need any footnotes. What were you thinking?

Measuring a company's worth on TAM or price-to-sales is dreaming poorly. Dreaming has to have a basis in reality. Otherwise, it really is just wishful thinking. Another example of dreaming poorly is doing so at others' expense. The Mag 7 companies have created new products and new ways of thinking. They have improved their customers' lives. I can't say the same thing about the vast majority of meme-based cryptocurrencies. We are in an era when "rug pulling" abounds. An excellent example of dreaming poorly, rug pulling is when a C-list celebrity starts a cryptocurrency, hoping to cash in on fleeting fame. A modern take on the classic fraud known as pump-and-dump, in the initial frenzied rush of investors, the originators sell out their stake and head for the hills with a bag of other people's money. No, that is decidedly not the way to dream. While Charles Ponzi's name lives on, it lives on in infamy. The purveyors of meme coins, non-fungible tokens, and bananas taped to the wall are unlikely to be granted even that level of notoriety. They will be forgotten as poor dreamers, if dreamers at all.

On the way back from Coney Island on my recent trip, I took a different line, the B train along the Brighton Line. This route is an open cut running north through Brooklyn. The trains run below street grade but out in the open with a clear, skylit view of everything coming down the track. From the front car, you see the towers of the Manhattan skyline looming in the distance and drawing inexorably closer with each stop. The route feels like a vital artery for the city, its passengers the critical oxygen needed to fuel its economy. As I looked around the car, I thought about my fellow passengers. Were they dreaming about what their commute would bring them, what their workdays would produce? I hoped so.

Every subway ride is an opportunity to dream, as is every trading day and every workday. As far as my own dreams, well, while I don't eat hot dogs anymore, I can attest that Nathan's crinkle-cut fries with ketchup taste as amazing as ever, especially walking down the boardwalk with the parachute drop looming over you. I'll dream of my next visit to Coney Island. I wish for you to take a subway ride and create your own dreams, too.

Photo Credit: Rhododendrites

Chapter 13

Balance, Harmony, Serenity

"TAKE THE TRAIN TO the plane, take the train to the plane."

In 1978, the Metropolitan Transportation Authority, operator of the New York City subways, and the Port Authority of New York and New Jersey, the operator of John F. Kennedy International Airport, joined forces to create a special subway line from Midtown Manhattan to JFK. The city's airports were notoriously difficult to get to. They were expensive to get to by cab, and driving thru Van Wyck Expressway traffic was no way to set the mood for a trip.

The JFK Express, with its catchy ad jingle, was worth a shot. The train ran on the existing 6th Avenue IND Line, with special cars, priority routing over other subways, and premium pricing. I remember my father taking the family on it once to get to the airport. Once. For all its aspirations, it was still the subway. A family of five full of luggage in those crime-ridden years made an awfully inviting target. I felt the danger acutely. We all did. The train did not even make it to the airport. At the Howard Beach subway stop you had to transfer to a bus that then took you to the airport. It was an underwhelming experience. Before long, the only people using it were ordinary workers willing to pay a premium for a faster commute from the outer neighborhoods. The service lost money and didn't last too long.

I've always thought it a major hit on New York City's reputation that it doesn't have easy subway service to any of its airports. The Chicago "El" rail line and the Washington Metro take you from their central business districts to O'Hare and Dulles airports with one-seat service. A few bucks is all it costs and it takes you right to the terminals. No messy transfers to a bus or internal tramway. Modern Asian and Middle Eastern airports are built from the ground up with mass transit to their metropolitan centers. Surely the greatest city in the world, the city that never sleeps, could figure out how to do the same?

So, give credit to New York City and its agencies for trying. And give them credit, too, for pulling the plug when it became clear it wasn't working. To achieve anything, you've got to take the risk of it not working out. Failed experiments in the NYC Subway include the skip-stop 1/9 service, in which the 7th Avenue IRT would alternate stations at which it stopped to speed travel along the route, and the Bowling Green–South Ferry Shuttle, which operated between two stations so close together that it was much faster to walk than ride. Along with the Train to the Plane, these have been consigned to the dustbin of history. So, too, have numerous abandoned subway stations over the years.

To receive rewards, you have to take risks. Along with the failures come the successes of the newest city subway line, the 2nd Avenue route, the first phase of which was finally placed into revenue service in 2017, forty-five years after it was begun. Or the extension of the Flushing 7 line to Manhattan's Far West Side, enabling an entirely new commercial and residential neighborhood to flourish where there once had been desolate rail yards.

So, too, in the stock market. You've got to take chances and, at the same time, you've got to realize that not all of your stock picks will work out. The art of selling is exactly that—an art. Investors speak of a "sell discipline." You can certainly set up rules of "If a stock goes down so many percent from where I purchased it, then I will automatically sell it. I can always buy it back." That only guarantees you will sell for lower than you purchased. My experience is that when people lose money on a stock, they are very unlikely to give it a second chance.

And the simple truth is, sometimes stocks and the stock market go down. Sometimes, also, the market's opinion of your stock is dead wrong. Sometimes, you're just supposed to hold on, even if the price action is making you think you made a mistake. No, the "sell discipline" is an art. The core of the art is asking yourself why your stock went down. Is there an overall market decline? Did it report an aberrationally bad quarter? Is it in a sector that is temporarily out of favor?

Those are all reasons for temporary losses, ones that can be reversed given the right amount of time.

But occasionally, what you thought you knew about a stock just isn't the case. It's in these cases that being brutally honest with yourself will keep you from creating your own Train to the Plane in your portfolio, an albatross that brings down your long-term return. I mentioned in an earlier chapter how Intel had lost its way. Boeing is another such example. To call Boeing a storied company is a gross understatement. This is the company that built the famous B-17 and B-29 bombers that helped the allies to win World War II. It ushered in the modern jet age of passenger travel with its 707 airliner and then expanded it further with the first jumbo jet, the 747, a.k.a. the Queen of the Skies. It has played a major role in every manned space program from NASA. Its engineering prowess is legendary.

I owned Boeing for several years, starting before the COVID-19 pandemic. A lot of problems came up along the way. The software it installed in the MAX version of its 737 workhorse jet liner was implicated in two fatal overseas crashes. The US and other governments grounded the plane while the problem was investigated. Then, the pandemic hit and global air travel ground to a halt. Airlines refused deliveries of planes. Production aircraft piled up on the tarmacs at Boeing's factories. It got to the point where employee parking lots were repurposed to store the unwanted planes.

In the defense and space business, things weren't going any better for Boeing. From 2022 to 2024, the company lost $10 billion in this segment. Much of the problem stemmed from fixed-price government contracts for which it had inadequately projected and priced in construction delays and cost overruns. But there were signs that the company's legendary engineering prowess was fading. Between the Boeing Starliner capsule for bringing astronauts to the International Space Station and the Space Launch System, NASA's rocket to send astronauts back to the moon and to Mars, Boeing couldn't get any of its vehicles off the ground, quite literally.

Still, the idea of a duopoly between Boeing and Airbus in commercial planes, and a tremendous backlog of government projects, kept me in the stock. I figured the company's mishaps were just a string of bad luck. That feeling vanished in January 2024 when an improperly installed panel blew out on an Alaska Airlines 737 in midflight. It was nothing short of a miracle that no one was killed and the plane was able to land safely. But for me, enough damage had been done. I was no longer willing to hold shares in a company where blind luck had prevented it from killing people. I sold my position in Boeing the next day.

The lesson in the Boeing saga is that the validity of your investment thesis in a company can change. When it does, and when that change is a negative, it is likely a reason to sell. Boeing's long history of aviation manufacturing excellence was undone by poor management. The company had made multiple acquisitions after the Cold War ended and military spending in the United States dramatically declined. None were bigger than the merger with another legendary aerospace company, McDonnell Douglas, in 1997. These mergers changed the managerial culture at Boeing. Profits became more important than quality. Quantity of planes out the door dominated concerns about safety. CEOs came and went with regularity, but the problems only grew. It took me a while to realize that fact. When the Alaska Airlines blowout made it undeniable, I sold. The original investment thesis, that Boeing was an engineering and manufacturing juggernaut, was no longer valid.

The sell discipline for an individual stock is different than that of selling "the market." Sometimes, I receive calls from clients made fearful by current events. That decision, to get out of the market entirely, is different than the decision to sell an individual stock. Here, too, there is an art to the process.

The worst thing an investment manager can do when advising clients is to get their risk tolerance wrong. Risk tolerance is a pretty ephemeral concept, one which the financial advisory industry has spent much time trying to quantify in an objective manner. Some of the measurement attempts are laughable. "What is the maximum amount of decline you are comfortable with in a market downturn?" is an example from a typical risk tolerance questionnaire. Zero is the right answer. Any client should be comfortable with zero declines in their portfolio. Yet, we know that markets will go down sometimes, and with them, our clients' accounts. We have to realistically assess our clients' ability to withstand those losses, temporary though they may be.

When I talk to clients, I tell them about the many catalysts for market declines that I have seen in my career. Some were legitimately terrifying. The Great Financial Crisis felt like the global financial system was ending and we were one misstep away from a Mesolithic barter economy. The economic shutdown associated with the COVID-19 pandemic is, obviously, another example. Others are supremely banal, or even inane. Quite often, a routine economic slowdown gets promoted in the press as auguring a new Great Depression, sentiments which in turn get amplified on social media, and lapped up by consumers. My favorite example of this was when the Bank of Cyprus froze depositors' accounts in 2013, leading to large losses for its customers. Its customers in Cyprus, that is. A country of less than one million inhabitants. And yet, coming close on the heels of the peripheral European debt crisis, which rocked the economies of Portugal, Italy, Ireland, Greece, and Spain into forced fiscal austerity, American financial markets took a tumble on the news. There was a shoot-first-ask-questions-later mentality at the time. This is the sort of event that has no lasting effect on financial markets yet, at the time, it did and it seemed monumental.

My goal in working with clients is to make sure to have the right perspective. Every downturn in the market has turned out to be a buying opportunity. No matter how incredible a current event seems, it is neither the first nor the last unprecedented event through which financial markets will persevere. Clients have finite lifespans, though, and I understand worries that a downturn may negatively impact near-term funding needs, be it kids' education, buying a house, or retirement and a reduction of income. Sometimes when I am asked to justify the fee that I charge for my services, I state emphatically that it is for keeping clients invested when their instinct is wrongly telling them to bail out of the markets.

Getting a client's ability to withstand market downturns is supremely important, though. The ramifications of getting it wrong can be dire. The worst outcome, and by extension the biggest failure of an investment advisor, is when clients call during a market rout saying "sell me out." The gravity of that mistake is often lost on them. They turn what history has shown time and time again to be a temporary loss and make it a permanent one.

A case in point is 2022, in which the S&P 500 closed down 19 percent and at one point fell below the bear market threshold of a more than 20 percent decline. For much of the year, I countered popular commentary by saying the market was getting it wrong: The much-ballyhooed recession it was predicting was unlikely to occur. The recession never did occur, and for that reason I refer to 2022 as a "faux bear market." I recall being on air one day in the last week of December and the lead story was "$10 Trillion Lost," as in that's how much money had been lost in the stock market that year. I couldn't go along with the theme, though, and pointed out that it's only lost if you sell. A great big argument ensued on live TV, but I was right. As I write this book, it is more than two years since that bear market. The S&P 500 gained more than 50 percent in that time frame. If you sold in 2022, you lost. If you held, you're near an all-time high.

Which leads to another good point: The market is always setting new highs. People often like to say, "How can I buy stocks with the stock market at an all-time high?" That's what the stock market does! It sets new highs, one after the other. That's the whole point, and it's been doing it for centuries! In this regard, I guess I take after my father and his parents before him. I listened to them speak to clients asking when was the right time to buy. The answer was and is, when you have the money to invest. If you are in this for the long run, time is an asset. The sooner you get invested, the more return you are likely to get over your lifetime. It is for this reason that when young adults ask me what's the first thing they should do in the markets, I tell them to maximize the amount they contribute to their 401(k)s and other retirement accounts. Combining a very long investment horizon with tax-deferred compounding is unbelievably powerful.

We've been living through many years in which political vitriol has increased exponentially, and with each election, both sides stoke the fear that the country is irretrievably changing for the worse. One day, perhaps, that will be true. While certainly aware of the risks, I don't see it that way. We live in an unbelievably vibrant country, with no close peers. And one of the many fabulous attributes of our country is the ability of ordinary citizens to enjoy the fruits of the country's success by investing in its stable, liquid, growing financial markets. You want to benefit financially from artificial intelligence, from life-saving drug discoveries, from enhanced access to outer space? All you have to do is invest in the stock market.

The point isn't that losses won't ever occur. Of course they will. But without taking the risk of a loss, you can't gain the reward of a return. Imagine if that first shovel at the City Hall subway station had never hit the ground.

The return from risk is not found just in the stock market; it is also found in the companies themselves. Starting a career is, in and of itself, a risk–return tradeoff. One can take a "safe" path that doesn't require much effort or ingenuity, but that often doesn't bring return. Taking the risk of diving into the unknown brings the potential for failure, though. Is it worth it?

I believe that Americans, generally speaking, love to dream. Over the years, I have been deeply enmeshed at three schools, one government agency, four corporations, and one national broadcast network. I began each of those adventures with high hopes and aspirations. I would cure cancer! I would become an admiral! I would be lauded as a CEO! That none of those original goals came to fruition does not make me feel like a failure. I learned lifelong lessons along the way. I wouldn't trade in any of those experiences. With them, I have achieved new goals that I couldn't have imagined in my youth.

I began at each of those eight institutions by leaving another one. Each of those transitions was fraught with risk. I was leaving the comfort of the known to embark upon a mysterious, indeterminate future. The potential for failure was ever present. You have to take those risks if you're going to make the most of yourself. Investing in the stock market is an excellent way to learn the balance between risk and reward in your life. It certainly benefited me.

Human evolution—human progress—is all about taking risks to improve the world. Okay, so the Train to the Plane now exists only in my head as a catchy tune. Too bad that it didn't work out. But its failure paved the way for improvement. The Port Authority of New York and New Jersey built the AirTrain to JFK Airport twenty-five years later. And the MTA built the East Side Access to allow Long Island Rail Road trains to get to Grand Central Terminal. It may not be the one-seat service of other cities, but New York now has a viable rail option to get from Midtown Manhattan to JFK. I know because I use it often. It's not bad at all!

Chapter 14

Gratitude

New York City is certainly one of the greatest cities in the world. Situated on a protected harbor with quick and direct access to transatlantic commerce, while also at the terminus of a major riverway into the Northeastern United States, its growth from the American Revolution to the twentieth century was rapid. Population grew by 50 percent every decade in the 1800s, culminating in 127 percent growth in the last decade of the century. A city that covered 1.5 square miles in 1800 grew to 91 square miles by 1900, and then to 3,353 square miles during the twentieth century. These statistics are just a few reasons why, to many, including me, New York is the greatest city in the world.

The need to move the city's population back and forth between work locations and residential centers that were becoming more and more distant was acute by the turn of the century. Horse-drawn carriages were slow and inefficient. Only a few passengers could be carried at a time. They were expensive, requiring both humans and horses to operate. The latter's detritus left undesirable messes all over the streets.

Elevated railways sprouted throughout the city in the second half of the nineteenth century. These solved the speed issue and allowed many more people to be transported at a time. However, these railways had their own downsides. The tracks blocked sunlight for the streets below. The steam-driven engines were noisy and dangerous to homes and businesses along the lines. Cinders from their fireboxes could be thrown from the smokestacks and cause fires. Smoke filled the apartments lining the tracks, causing health problems, particularly for children. For a city still reeling from journalist Jacob Riis's photo series on poverty and squalor, New York could not stand for the situation as it was.

Running electrified trains underground seemed a good solution to the problem. And yet, from the passage of the Rapid Transit Act in 1894 that got the ball rolling, it took six more years for the first contract to be awarded, and another four until the first line was opened. In the intervening time period, the prospective subway became the target of lawsuits that held up progress. Not in My Backyard (NIMBY) protesters did all they could to obstruct what were destined to become pieces of infrastructure critical to New York's development into a world-class metropolis. Claims of infringement on constitutional property rights, damage from noise and pollution, and even doubting the city's sovereignty were brought forth. Economically and efficiently laid-out rights of way had to be rerouted. Costs went up and construction was delayed. Eventually, the first subway line was completed and, when it met with great success, others quickly followed. The city got the critical infrastructure it needed and its progress as the nation's biggest metropolis continued.

It is amusing to think that in the modern era, easy access to subway stations is considered a plus by both businesses and residences. Funny how it goes sometimes. What one thinks may be a travesty turns out to be a wonderful thing. This concept is writ large in the stock market. I always chuckle at those who talk only about their investment successes. Nobody likes to talk about their mishaps, making it seem like they have a blemish-free track record though we all know nobody bowls a perfect game in the stock market. It's the losses, the mistakes, the lessons learned the hard way that make an investor. It's what opens one's eye to new under-valued investment opportunities. It's what makes a person's character worthy, as well. In fact, I strongly believe we should be grateful for the events in life that knock us down. They inevitably lead to greater future success than we would have had without them.

Consider this little anecdote. Not that long ago I was scrolling through YouTube videos. Who knows what I was looking for. Probably submarine documentaries. Whatever I clicked on started with a commercial first. It was the kind you can skip after ten seconds, but I found myself engrossed by it. It was a testimonial of a woman telling what she went through in the Great Financial Crisis of 2008 to 2009. She had recently retired and was living off her 401(k), only to see its value cut in half in the space of a few months. The fear that she felt as the markets went down hard was palpable. I felt her anxiety. To this day, I'm not sure what the product was in the commercial. I think it was a pitch for some investment trading strategy. I couldn't focus on the rest of the commercial because all I could do was mutter to myself "Please don't tell me you sold" over and over again as it ran.

In March 2009, at the nadir of the Great Financial Crisis, the S&P 500 bottomed out at 666. In the sixteen years since then, it is up nine-fold, for an annualized return of 15 percent. To be fair to the protagonist in the commercial, perhaps it is better to measure from the market apex that preceded the 60 percent crisis-induced decline. In October 2008, the S&P 500 topped out at 1,576. Since that point, it is up almost four times, for a 9 percent annualized return. From either starting point, it has been a heroic run, one that far outstrips cash, investment grade bonds, and all measures of inflation. All that poor lady had to do was not sell. I know, in either measuring period, the horror of the recession and bear market loomed large. Terrible events can and often do lead to great outcomes in investing.

Some people will go through a bear market and swear off stocks forever. It happened to my paternal grandparents who started a municipal bond firm in 1925 only to face the stock market crash of 1929 that ushered in the Great Depression of the 1930s. Not a great time to start up a financial services firm. I never got to know my grandfather, who passed away from a stroke in 1951. But everyone in my family knew and respected his wife, Sayra, who ran the firm for the forty years after that. For decades she was the Lebenthal family matriarch. From her we learned everything financial, whether it was how to endorse a check or how to clip coupons on a bond (yes, there actually used to be physical coupons that represented your interest payments and they were attached to a physical certificate to document your ownership of municipal debt).

When she found out that I had a predilection for investing in stocks, she did not express outright disapproval. But from this woman who lived into her nineties, with decades of experience in finance, I never once received her thoughts on a stock. She had sworn off them after the Great Depression.

I consider it a shame when that happens to people. When held for the long run, stocks are a fabulous investment. Of course they sometimes go down. Volatility and risk are the price of admission. But given long-term returns like those from before and after the Great Financial Crisis, staying invested is a marvelous thing, a gift for which one can give thanks. I believe the biggest benefit I can give my clients as their advisor is to hold their hands during rough market times. To make sure they recognize that the bad times don't last, and that on the other side of them lie meaningful gains.

I think about being grateful through hard times a lot. Maybe it surprises you to hear me say that. Many people think I was born with a silver spoon in my mouth. While I lived a comfortable middle-class life growing up, the most important things my parents gave to me were a quality education and a ton of drive. Whatever else the public perceives to be a privileged background did not grant me success in the Navy, or admission to the top business school, or a job at Goldman Sachs, or a coveted recurring spot on CNBC.

Those sorts of things are not given. They are earned. And with the successes I have had, let me tell you, I have had plenty of times where I felt my world was ending.

One incident from the Navy stands out. Most of my first two years consisted of training. There's a lot of learning that goes into being a naval officer, a nuclear engineer, and a submariner. Officer Candidate School was a four-month boot camp, complete with the first-day head shave, Marine Corps drill sergeants screaming in your face, and being woken up by trombones blown into your face. After that was a full year's worth of learning the physics and practice of naval reactors, followed by three months of Submarine School. Each stage was intense and fully immersive. The training consumed you day and night, through the weekends and holidays.

It was during the nuclear engineering training that a seminal moment occurred. For the first year, I had excelled. I graduated in the top 10 percent of Officer Candidate School, earning a commission in the "regular" Navy as opposed to being on active reserve. That was a distinction without a difference, as everyone was a full-time, war-fighting officer. Still, I was proud and honored to be part of one of our nation's finest institutions, and in distinguished standing. Six months of classroom nuclear engineering training followed. Masters-level courses in thermodynamics, chemistry, particle physics, metallurgy, and math were fed to us at a firehose pace. Again, I was proud to end up in the top 10 percent of the class.

Then followed what is known as Prototype. Prototype is six more months of nuclear engineering school, but this time in operation of a real, live, naval nuclear reactor. The Navy had four such Prototype sites established: Idaho, New York, Charleston, and Connecticut. I was assigned to the S1C reactor in Windsor, Connecticut, in September 1991. What followed was one of the darkest and coldest winters of my life.

Windsor is located in the heart of New England a few miles north of Hartford, Connecticut's capital. It is a strange place to have a naval facility, twenty-five miles inland from the nearest seashore. Very few residents then (or now) knew that there was a fully operational nuclear reactor in their midst. To properly train nuclear engineers, the Navy had built a mockup of a submarine hull with a first-generation propulsion plant within. The plant operated almost continuously in six-hour shifts. As officers, we trained in leading the watchstanding crew of enlisted men in starting up and shutting down the reactor, running it at power as if at sea, performing maintenance on it, and, most important, running casualty drills.

Casualty drills were simulated emergencies, such as fire, flooding, loss of reactor cooling, radioactivity releases, and so on. The Navy had devised procedures for many different things that could go wrong. Several of these were learned through real-life lessons of when things do go wrong. Three Mile Island and Chernobyl provided plenty of examples of unexpected failures. There were more, less-publicized, events from the early history of US nuclear power in the 1950s and 1960s. The 1961 SL-1 incident from the National Reactor Testing Station in Idaho is a great example. The SL-1 was part of the US Army's research into smaller reactors that might be used to power remote bases. It had control rods used to moderate fissioning uranium atoms and these rods were manipulated by hand. When, one day during maintenance, an operator pulled too hard on a stuck rod, it jumped an extra foot, resulting in a power surge that blew the reactor apart. Three men were killed, and so much radioactive contamination was released that a responding ambulance had to be abandoned and buried afterwards. There are more gruesome details that you can look up online. The point is, from the SL-1 incident many lessons were learned. These included that control rods were far too sensitive to be moved manually. Many of the casualty procedures that we practiced in the nuclear navy involved stuck rods or ones that were moving inappropriately.

Life at S1C in many ways felt like it was out of the 1960s, as well. To be specific, it felt like it belonged in the Cold War parody movie *Dr. Strangelove*. To begin with, for all the technological prowess represented by nuclear power, the base was a mess. Ancient-looking derricks, water towers, and other infrastructure made for a steam-punk feel without the charm. The buildings were rundown. They had the feeling of a truck stop well past its prime. I remember doing classwork in rooms with leaking roofs. The cafeteria where we ate most of our meals specialized mostly in fried foods. Soldiers toting M-16s continually patrolled the ground. It felt like living in a black-and-white movie.

Barely more than a year removed from the ivy-covered gothic charm of Princeton, I was not yet fully adjusted to my new life in the Navy. Every so often I would visit New York City to see how my former classmates were faring. With most of them at investment banks or consulting firms, they were wrapped up in their own immersive programs, but when I did see them the contrast between their worlds and mine was stark. I found myself getting a little homesick.

It took time to get the hang of the training at S1C. This was no longer book-learning. It was real-world reactor plant operations. It involved crucial management of enlisted people, some of whom resented the college-educated officers in charge. If they could help one of us to slip up, that garnered currency among their brethren. The transient nature of the many trainees going through the training pipeline did not engender the almost family-like affinity among officers and crew contained in a sea-going submarine. It was at this time that I had a significant slip-up.

The goal of Prototype was to get qualified to run naval nuclear reactors. With this, you could actually matriculate to an ocean-going assignment. To qualify, you have to stand before a board of senior naval nuclear officers while running the plant through normal operations and casualty drills. It was a pressure cooker. The enlisted men could not help you, nor could the instructors. It was meant to create the crucible of being on your own as the Engineering Officer of the Watch in a submarine actually at sea.

As mentioned, S1C was an early submarine reactor. It had many quirks in its design that, once put into operation, were found out to be inefficient and non-intuitive to its operators. It was a tough plant to master, and certainly a bear for a new ensign to cut his teeth on. I did not do well on the qualification watch. Many alarm bells, warning lights, and shouted reports fired off during the casualties and I didn't recognize what they meant. Steps in the procedures fled my mind as the tension built. Sweat beads formed on my brow and my orders were clipped and nonsensical. I was missing things, important things. My field of view narrowed into tunnel vision. The enlisted men started turning around at their watchstations to watch the ensign go down in flames. At the end, the commanding officer of the plant came to me and said, "You're not going to like this." I had failed. Not gotten a bad grade. Full-on flunked.

This moment had potentially severe ramifications. In the nuclear navy, failure is not trivial. This was not a situation of going to see a professor or teaching assistant for make-up tests. The old man, Admiral Rickover himself, had purposely designed the training program to be hard. He wanted to make sure that his fleet of nuclear-powered submarines, aircraft carriers, and cruisers would have a blemish-free track record. He has succeeded, four decades after his departure. There have been no major reactor accidents in the US Navy since its inception. My failure created the significant possibility of my getting booted from the nuclear program. Like the woman who watched her 401(k) become a 201(k) during the Great Financial Crisis, my mind took over and went to dark places.

Would I be allowed to continue as an officer of the line, even aboard conventionally powered surface ships? What standing would I have in that case? I imagined being assigned to a transport ship plying the trade routes, rarely doing anything exciting for the remaining years on my contract. What would my friends and family say? My decision to forego continuing my molecular biology undergraduate degree by signing up for the Navy was not initially met with a round of applause by family and friends. While some had come around to its appeal, would that remain if I failed to qualify for nuclear-powered submarines?

That evening, I lay on my bed, catatonic. My roommates, several of whom I had been together with since boot camp, nervously checked in on me to see if I was okay. I had been regarded as a bit of a "golden child" to that moment. Therein lay the problem. I had been promoted through the training program faster than I should have. There was a clear gap between book learning and practical smarts in running a reactor plant. It was a gap I had not leapt across. I needed help, from my fellow officers, and especially from the enlisted men with whom I worked. I realized the antagonism that I had felt from them was perceived as a two-way street. Many of them found me haughty and unapproachable. And perhaps I was. A severe attitude correction was called for. I recognized it and met the challenge head-on.

I brought myself back to the plant and dove in with renewed vigor. I engaged with my crewmates and learned the ropes. Above all else, I carried myself with humility. The drive to succeed was still there, but I harnessed it with more empathy for those around me. I admitted what I didn't know and asked for help. Life is not a fairytale, but in this case, things ended better than I could have hoped. I was re-examined by the qualification board and passed easily. I had a few oral and written exams that went well, too. When all was said and done, that same commanding officer presented me with the Honorman award for graduating at the top of my class.

Words can't do justice to the experience of my six months at Prototype. It was cold and I felt like a fish out of water. From that discomfort came a lifelong lesson: I know a heck of a lot less than I think I do. Let me qualify that. I have plenty of opinions. I make projections about what the future will hold. It is vital to do that in investing and in life. But the things I know with absolute certainty are much fewer than I think. For that reason, I've learned to be up-front and say when I don't know. This is true when I am asked about an investment or a business decision. There is little that is knowable in an absolute sense about the future. For this reason, when someone tells you that his model of a stock, the economy, or the universe gives a 100 percent chance of something happening, you should run the other way from that person. They may turn out to be right. That's not the point. It's the lack of intellectual honesty that inevitably leads to failure, as it did during my first qualification watch at S1C.

I am grateful for the experience I had and the lessons I learned the hard way at Prototype. It wasn't fun at all. Being grateful under all circumstances is a character trait I continually work on. It is especially important when things go wrong. An investment thesis blows up in your face and clients are mad at you. A business opportunity fades away before it can be acted on. Someone crosses you with a bad word. More often than not, something good comes from it. At the very least, every experience is a chance to learn. It's just like the store owners when the original subway line was built at their front door. Worried about loss of business, they eventually found that droves of potential customers were now within reach of their wares.

There are plenty of times I enter the subway, late to get to the Stock Exchange for my CNBC appearance, only to find a delay. Track maintenance, police activity, or maybe even no announced reason at all. Instead of getting frustrated and anxious, I remind myself how many things have gone right in my life and how much I have to be grateful for. I will admit, there are plenty of times when I'm hit by a curveball and I've got to work really, really hard to remain grateful. It has to be a lifelong mindset. I don't know much, but I'm convinced that gratitude as a way of life is the only way to live.

Epilogue

I'VE WRITTEN THIS BOOK with a strong element of casting caution to the wind. It has been an opportunity to share with you something that is important to me, the New York City Subway system, and tie it to other vital aspects of my being: the stock market and my business career. Had I played it safe, I would have just written about the latter two topics. Instead, I've invited you to discover a hidden side of my life, this fascination with New York's underground railway system.

There's risk in exposing myself like this. Undoubtedly, there will be people who read this and think what an absolute clown Jim Lebenthal is. I can picture the usual suspects who might do so right now, although I won't give them the satisfaction of jotting down their names. Putting oneself out there is a risk. But not doing so, and keeping bottled up inside this passion of mine, seems a greater risk. A risk to my own self-esteem. I'm proud of who I am. Life has given me enough setbacks to carry myself with humility, but I've dedicated myself to my professional pursuits. I want to share them with you. And, as I've mentioned several times in this book, without risk you forego reward.

There's another type of risk that I've taken in this book. You've probably noticed that a few of the stock examples I've used are still playing out. The safe way to write this book would have been to only include stock stories where the end has already been reached: I've bought, held, and sold. Intel, Boeing, GM are such examples. But in the case of Transocean or Cleveland-Cliffs, I'm still holding the shares, even as the book goes to print. Who knows? Maybe I'll be proven right in my theses on these names, or maybe I'll be shown to be a fool. That's the nature of every investment, although with this book there will be an indelible record for posterity. A good friend once told me: You don't buy securities, you sell securities. What you buy are *in*securities. When you sell a stock, you know all you're going to know about the company, the good, the bad, and the ugly. When you buy one, however, you're taking the risk that it won't work out, no matter how good your investment analysis is.

That is the story of life. It is unpredictable. It is uncontrollable. It can be fun and exhilarating, and it can make you feel downtrodden. And the same can be said for each and every subway ride that you take. I expect to discover something exciting every time I walk down the stairs into the subway system. I also know that things can go wrong. There may be an equipment failure or, worse, I might have a scary encounter. The subway does have its collection of unique characters, not all of whom have my best interests at heart. Again, true in the stock market where on the other side of every trade is a counter-party taking the exact opposite view, and whose economic interest is tied to you being wrong.

The same is true every day of business life. In my particular version of the corporate world, I advise clients on their finances. There are many, many ways in which my advice can change a family's economic well-being. Every decision I make carries the risk that it can go awry and damage a client's financial well-being. That risk can't stop me from making that decision. Herewith comes a somewhat odd observation. Often when a Ponzi scheme, such as the one run by Bernie Madoff, is brought to light, there is a subtext to the story: The manager who engaged in the fraud often admits to being paralyzed in making investment decisions. It isn't just a case of bad trades that lost money. It's often no trades made at all. Wouldn't the decision to buy a few stocks have been made more easily when deciding to hoodwink clients? Making no trades seems not only harder but destined to be inevitably discovered.

In a less scurrilous sense, the decisions I make on a daily basis also carry the risk that someone else out there is doing it better. Competition is ever present in any industry. At any moment, on any day, I may receive a call from a client notifying me that my services are no longer required and he is moving to another advisor. I've managed that risk by noting two facts. First, my business has only grown over time. And second, the clients that have stayed with me over the years tend to be those who understand fully my investing methodology. Again, risk carries with it the seeds of reward.

I'll be incautious in a different way by highlighting a huge mistake the New York City Metropolitan Transportation Authority has made over the past few decades. The subways need to be advertised. They are too easily taken for granted by the city's residents. Even worse, they can easily be vilified. A crime streak in the subway wreaks havoc on the hearts and minds of its riders. Unfortunately, they have occurred again and again in my lifetime. Add to that the costs. Not just the fares, but the taxes that are paid to meet the system's perennial operating deficit. New York recently became the first city to institute congestion pricing, charging cars a tax to drive into Manhattan. The proceeds will go to financial support for the subways. This idea has not gone over well with the public, who perceive it as a money grab.

Yes, the MTA has made a mistake over the past many years by not properly marketing the subway. One of the easiest fixes is right in front of everyone's faces. The windows in the front of the train, the ones I used to love to look through, for which I demanded my parents always take the first car so I could see down the tracks, are no longer available to common mortals. Years ago, the decision was made to expand the train operator's cab from a small booth on one side of the car all the way across the width of the train. Now, that window in the front car looks into the motorman's cab. You have to look through the motorman's cab and through *his* windshield to see down the tunnel. And for some inexplicable reason, the first window is made opaque, giving a fuzzy view of the track. By doing this, the MTA has removed its best advertisement. Young children simply cannot see from the front of the train. There is no more "coldest eyeball in New York City." Do we wonder why some youths are now enthralled with "subway surfing" on top of the cars? Give them their front-window view back! Get the children revved up to ride the subways again. It is the best possible advertising for this incredible asset to the city.

One of the best parts of being a subway lover is the ability to further enjoy the many cities around the world with their urban rail transits. Chicago's El, San Francisco's BART, Boston's T. And the international systems: Paris's Metro with its distinctive rubber-tire clad trains, London with the original Tube. A few years ago, I did the most un-Los Angeles thing while in LA: I took the light-rail transit from Santa Monica to visit the Battleship USS Iowa Museum in Long Beach. It was a little crazy, a little dangerous, and incredibly fun. I saw parts and people of the city that I never would have from an Uber. I highly recommend checking out any city you are in by using the subway system to travel.

Even more important, the subway can draw us all together. That may sound a little goofy, but recently I was skiing in Zermatt, Switzerland. On one of the trains up the mountain (yes, a train took us up the mountain—the Swiss have alpine railroads in their blood), a group of fellow travelers and I noticed that we all had cell phone cases with New York City Subway MetroCards in the pouches. It was an instant bonding moment.

As I draw our journey to a close, more than anything, I hope I have inspired you to view the extraordinary in what you might otherwise consider the monotony of life. Millions of people ride the New York City Subway every day. Imagine if every one of them on every day felt the awe of it that I've expressed in these pages. Imagine the energy, the creativity, and the positivity that would be created.

With that, I thank you profusely for riding the rails of these pages with me. This has been a marvelous journey that we took together!

THE AUTHOR IS EMPLOYED by and a partner at Cerity Partners, LLC, an SEC-registered investment adviser. As required by the firm's compliance policies, this manuscript was submitted to the firm's compliance department for regulatory review only. The review was limited solely to ensuring the author's compliance with securities regulations applicable to registered persons, the author's duty to the firm regarding confidential and proprietary information and the firm's policies on outside business activities. The review by Cerity Partners, LLC did not constitute editorial control or input, endorsement of the book's content, views, or recommendations by Cerity Partners, approval or adoption of the book as firm marketing material or review or verification of the accuracy of statements or strategies discussed. The views and strategies presented are those of the author alone and may differ from those of Cerity Partners, LLC.